S0-AYC-646

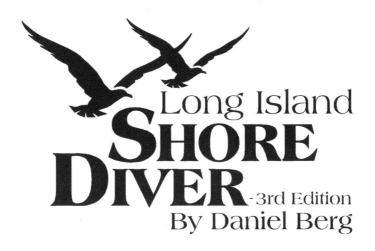

Long Island
SHORE
DIVER -3rd Edition
By Daniel Berg

THE DIVER'S GUIDE TO
LONG ISLAND, N.Y. BEACH DIVING SITES

Contributing Writer, Denise Berg

DISCLAIMER

Please be aware that the information contained in this book is only a supplement to proper diving instruction. Reading this book does not qualify a diver to do dives or to participate in any activity beyond the capabilities of his own qualifications experience and training.

Please use the information contained within this book as a basic guideline. Let good diving skills, common sense, and courtesy lead you and your dive buddy to safely enjoy exploring Long Island's coast.

Library of Congress Catalog Card No.00 092808
ISBN:0-9707067-0-7

FOR ADDITIONAL COPIES, WRITE TO:

AQUA EXPLORERS, INC.
980 Church St
Baldwin NY 11510
Phone/Fax (516) 868-2658
E-Mail: Wreckvalle@aol.com
Web Page: www.AquaExplorers.com

ABOUT THE
AUTHOR

Capt. Dan Berg is a P.A.D.I. (Professional Association of Diving Instructors) Master Scuba Diver Trainer. He is a Specialty Instructor in Wreck Diving, Night Diving, Search and Recovery, Underwater Hunting, Deep Diving, Dry Suit Diving, U/W Metal Detector Hunting, U/W Archeology, and has written and teaches his own nationally approved Distinctive Specialties in Shipwreck Research, Shipwreck Sketching and U/W Cinematography. Dan also holds certifications in Rescue, U/W photography, Medic First Aid, Oxygen Administration and Environmental Marine Ecology. Dan is a US Coast Guard licensed Master and a member of the Eastern Dive Boat Association. He owns and operates his own 40' charter dive boat Wreck Valley, which runs out of Jones Inlet on Long Islands South Shore. Mr. Berg holds four US Patents for Scuba Equipment Design. Dan is the author of over 10 books including the original WRECK VALLEY book, a record of shipwrecks off Long Island's South Shore, SHORE DIVER, a diver's guide to Long Island's beach sites, WRECK VALLEY Vol II, a record of shipwrecks off Long Island's South Shore and New Jersey, co-author of TROPICAL SHIPWRECKS, a vacationing diver's guide to the Bahamas and Caribbean, BERMUDA SHIPWRECKS, a vacationing diver's guide to Bermuda's shipwrecks, SHIPWRECK DIVING, a complete diver's handbook to mastering the skills of wreck diving, FLORIDA SHIPWRECKS, the diver's guide to shipwrecks around the state of Florida and the Florida keys, NEW JERSEY BEACH DIVER, The Diver's guide to New Jersey Beach Diving Sites, and the LONG ISLAND SHORE DIVER, The diver's guide to Long Island, NY beach diving sites. Mr. Berg was the executive producer and host of the DIVE WRECK VALLEY CABLE television series, which aired for eight consecutive years on MSG, SPORTSCHANNEL, and nationally on the OUTDOOR CHANNEL. His award winning underwater cinematography has been used on a variety of other TV shows, including LONG ISLAND ALL OUTDOORS, LONG ISLAND FISHING, FOX 5 NEWS, CBS NEWS, EYE WITNESS NEWS, NEWS 12 and DIVER'S DOWN. Dan's photographs and shipwreck articles have been published in SKIN DIVER MAGAZINE, UNDERWATER USA, NAUTICAL BRASS, The FISHERMAN MAGAZINE, FISHEYE VIEW MAGAZINE, SHIPWRECKS, NAUTILUS, EASTERN & WESTERN TREASURES, THE SUB AQUA JOURNAL, SHIPS AND SHIPWRECKS, NEW JERSEY WRECK DIVER, FIRE ISLAND TIDE, TREASURE MAGAZINE plus many more.*

Photo by Mike McMeekin

ACKNOWLEDGEMENTS

I would like to thank the following for their time, knowledge and information: First, my wife Denise for the hours she spent re-writing and proof reading; and Jozef Koppelman, who spent countless hours in the water with his cameras. Captain Steve Bielenda, Mel Brenner, Randi Eisen, Captain Hank Garvin, Aaron Hirsh, Captain John Lachenmayer, Pete Nawrocky, Janice Raber, Bruce Raden, Herb Segars, Phil Senk, Darryl Steinhauser, Ed Tiedemann, Jeanne Tiedemann, Also my diving partners, Steve Jonassen, Ed Slater, Captain Rick Schwarz and Mike McMeekin. I am also grateful to my father Winfred Berg for his continued support, and my brother Donald Berg for his technical advice. Without the assistance and dedication of all listed, this text would not have been possible.

UNDERWATER PHOTOGRAPHY

I would like to acknowledge and sincerely thank the following for their beautiful underwater photographs. A picture is worth a thousand words, and the photos taken by these professionals capture all the beauty, mystery, thrill and excitement of diving off Long Island's beaches. I am grateful to Jozef Koppelman, Pete Nawrocky, Rick Schwarz, Randi Eisen and Herb Segars.

HOW TO USE

All the beach sites listed within this text are complete with directions and dive conditions. The easiest way to choose a site is to decide what part of Long Island you want to visit. After deciding this, reference the map in front of the book to get the closest sites. Next, read about each site and decide which one meets your dive objectives or experience level. The directions given are from a main thoroughfare, so, depending on your location, they might not be the most direct routes. Please look at a map to obtain the best possible connecting route; then proceed, following the printed directions in this text.

Please note that this book is not a complete listing of all Long Island beach sites. I would like to ask divers to contact the publisher with any additional information so that we may update the text accordingly at the next printing.

While reading this book, keep in mind that some locations are known by different names. I have listed most of these names in the index, which is found in the back of the book.

Directions, parking, dive conditions, or even the legality of diving a particular site could change. Please use the information contained within this book only as a basic guideline, and let good diving skills, common sense, and courtesy lead you to enjoy Long Island's great beach diving.

Long Island
SHORE
DIVER

Connecticut

Long Island

SHORE DIVER

1) Atlantic Beach Bridge	17) Atlantic Beach Bridge	33) Laurel Lake
2) Atlantic Beach Jetty	18) Done Deal	34) Long Beach
3) Atlantic Beach OldBridge	19) Duck Pond Point	35) Luce Landing
4) Bannister Creek Barge	20) Dutch Springs	36) Makamah
5) Bayville Barge & Sub	21) Eatons Neck Barge	37) Manhattan Beach
6) Bayville Beach	22) Fort Pond Bay	38) Mattituck Jetties
7) Beach 6th-9th Street	23) Garveys Jetty	39)Montauk Jetties
8) Beach 59th Street Wreck	24) Garveys Mooring Area	40) Moriches Jetty
9) Black Banks	25) Greenport Bridge	41) Murphy Wreck
10) Caumsett State Park	26) Greenport Jetty	42) OBI Beach
11) Cedar Beach & Jetties	27) Hempstead Harbor Park	43) USS Ohio
12) Center Island Beach	28) Horton Point	44) Old Ferry Pier
13) Clarkes Beach	29) Island Park Beach	45) Old Ponquogue Bridge
14) H.M.S. Culloden	30) Jones Beach Jetty	46) Paradise Cove
15) Cupsoque Beach Park	31) Kenneys Road Beach	47) Roanoke Point Barges
16) Democrat Point	32) Lake Ronkonkoma	48) Rocky Point East

49) Rocky Point Landing	
50) Roda Wreck	
51) Rye Cliff Ferry	
52) Sag Harbor Jetties	
53) Sea Cliff Beach	
54) Shell Creek	
55) Shinnecock Jetties	
56)Shoreham Jetties	
57) Sore Thumb	
58) Summerville Tug	
59) Teddy Roosevelt Park	
60) Throgs Neck Jetty	
61) Weaks Point Jetty	
62) Wildwood Lake	

New Jersey

N

DIVING TIPS

Over the years divers have developed or applied techniques and used certain pieces of equipment to make the sport easier, more enjoyable and safer. Here are a few tips that you might find useful:

SAFETY

A non-diver who comes along for the trip will not only be able to help divers with equipment, but should be informed as to the complete dive plan and plan of action if divers do not return on schedule. This beach buddy also should be informed of the diver OK and distress signals.

On remote beaches, a hand-held marine radio or CB will be very useful in case of an emergency.

Always leave word at home where you will be diving.

A small first aid kit to manage minor cuts and bruises should be assembled and brought on every dive.

SUITING UP

Sand causes the most aggravation to beach divers, as it seems to get everywhere, such as into wet suits, regulators, "O" rings, etc. To reduce the amount of sand getting into your gear, either suit up out of a car or bring a large plastic tarp to stand on. I also would suggest bringing a bucket and filling it with water before the dive. This way, after the dive, sand can be quickly removed from your feet by stepping into the bucket before stepping back onto the tarp.

Some wet suits, especially rented ones are often very difficult to get into. A trick that was shown to me by my instructor was to mix up a solution of 75% water and 25% liquid soap and keep it readily available in a small squeeze bottle. This solution not only helps divers slip into their suits, but cleans the suit as well.

On cold and windy days, especially while diving in the winter, use your car or other structure as a wind barrier while suiting up or un-suiting.

Bringing a thermos filled with warm water, and pouring some into your gloves or wet suit boots will help take the chill off after a cold-water dive. Re-usable chemical heat packs also will come in very handy when trying to get rid of a chill.

DIVING

Once in the water, especially when diving a new location, take a compass bearing straight out from the beach. This basic navigational information allows the diver to swim out and enjoy the dive, while always knowing at least the basic direction the shore is in. Divers can then swim on a reciprocal course that should bring them back to shore without ever having to surface for directions. Once practiced, this underwater navigation technique should become almost second nature while diving. As another navigational aid, divers should count the number of kick cycles it takes them to swim out. With this count, divers then know the approximate number of kick cycles it will take to return to shore, not compensating for any current.

If a boat engine is heard while you are submerged, lie flat on the bottom, if possible, next to a big rock until the sound fades. Do not surface to see where the boat is until you are sure it's safe.

A diver can flash his light, or tap with the butt of a knife on his own tank to get the attention of his buddy, or other divers. Buddies who dive together should attempt better underwater communications through hand signals or by talking through their regulators. Talking through your regulator takes some practice, but after awhile you and your buddy will understand what is being said. I have communicated this way in zero visibility when hand signals are of no use.

If you should locate a new wreck, or site that you want to return to, swim to the surface and while staying directly over the site, take compass bearings of two objects on the beach. Use objects that are permanent, easy to see, and far enough apart to create about a 90 degree angle.

This double compass course called triangulation is very accurate. If no compass is available, line up two objects on the beach. For example, a telephone pole lined up with the left side of a house. Whatever your land bearings or land ranges are, draw out a little map. This way, years down the line, you will still be able to find the same spot without having to rely on memory.

When trying to find any of the wrecks off the coast most divers usually find it easier to navigate out with a compass. If the wreck is not located, the divers surface to check their land bearings. Recently, diver Dan Lieb told me another technique he uses to locate a wreck. Dan recommends swimming out on the surface. The diver holds his dive flag that has a weighted line attached. The weight can be made of sinkers and does not have to be too heavy. While on the surface, the diver swims out to the site. Once he passes over the wreck the weighted line bounces and catches into the wreck. The diver then swims down and secures his flag line to the wreck and begins to explore. Mr Lieb reports that this method saves on air and allows divers to use land ranges while swimming out to a site.

NIGHT DIVING

Night divers, or any diver for that matter, should never shine a dive light directly into anyone else's eyes. Doing so will ruin or reduce night vision.

Night diving can be very productive, especially when searching for lobsters. Divers should bring at least two lights plus attach a cylume light stick to their regulator yoke. This chemical light stick enables dive teams to stay in contact with each other by monitoring the cylume light stick's glow.

Navigation back to shore can be made relatively easy by leaving a blinking light, similar to a road hazard light, on shore before entering the water. This light then gives divers a distinct point to navigate back to after their dive. Believe me, at night the entire coast could look remarkably similar, and this light should prevent some long walks back to your entry point.

UNDERWATER HUNTING

Night is definitely the best time to catch the nocturnal lobster. These tasty crustaceans also can be found during the day by searching through holes that are found in jetties and wrecks, etc. A strong, narrow beam dive light is the best type of light to use when trying to see deep inside these small caves.

Divers in search of dinner often ignore mussels, but they shouldn't be, as they are very tasty. Collect mussels from mid-water where they are rinsed constantly by the tide. They will be clean and tender. Mussels clinging to poles near the surface in the sunlight will not be as tender. Mussels picked from the bottom will be full of sand or mud.

Spear fishing should only be done in clear water. Always make sure you can see the full distance of your shot. For example, don't use an eight-foot cord in four-foot visibility, as you could accidentally hit another diver. To spear a fish, swim slowly without making any quick movements, and try for a shot just behind the head. If hit in the stomach, the fish could spin off the spear, while if hit in the head, the spear could just bounce off.

EXPLORING NEW DIVE SITES

This book has by no means listed every beach dive on Long Island. I have listed all the sites, which I have been to over the years, or have had knowledge of. There are still miles and miles of unexplored waterfront along both the north and south shores.

The first thing to do when trying to locate a new dive site is to decide your dive objectives. For example, if you are only interested in catching lobsters, you must look for rocks, a wreck, a jetty, or some other obstruction where they are known to make their home. If your objective were to find old bottles, a good place to look would be at old fishing piers, or anywhere else that people would drink and discard bottles. If you were interested in underwater photography, you would, of course, want marine life and good visibility.

Let's use the example of a diver who wants to find a new bottling site. First get some old marine charts or maps. You will be amazed at how much information they contain. Look for dump sites, ferry piers, etc., and mark them down. Next, look on an up-to-date street map for basic directions. Then you have to do some leg work, and drive to the sites to see if they are accessible. Sometimes there won't be any parking, or a site will be located on private property, but when you do get in the water at a new site, it can be quite rewarding.

In general, the north shore offers a better beach dive. Close to shore is a sand bottom, where visibility can be very good, and rocks are found scattered all along the coast. The south shore's inland bays have more of a silty mud bottom. The inlets and jetties on the south shore do have sand bottoms and are nice, but most of them have strong currents. Also, a lot of south shore beach-front is private property, or public beaches, which makes them hard to get to. Some other new dive sites, which may open in the future, include additional state parks. Currently, with the exception of Caumsett Park and a few others, state parks do not allow scuba diving. However, state owned lands might soon be open to the sport diving public. These waterfront parks will offer divers more unexplored coasts for fun and recreation.

To recap, after you pick your dive objective, a little research or planning will usually yield more rewards than trial and error.

TIDES AND CURRENTS

It is extremely important that divers understand the fundamentals before diving in any type of current. Currents are caused by tides, wind, weather and waves. These mass movements of water can sometimes be powerful and should not be underestimated.

On the north shore of Long Island divers will mostly notice a mild tidal drift. This type of water movement may not be very swift, but divers must still make a mental note of the general direction so they can compensate when navigating back to shore. Divers also should try to start their dive by swimming into or against the current. This way, at the end of the dive, the current will assist the dive team in returning to their entry point.

On the north and south shore, when there is an inlet involved, or whenever a large volume of water is moving through a narrow space during either a Flood or Ebb Tide, the force will be strong. When diving in or around areas that have Rip Currents, divers should realize that the current will disperse after it has passed through the funnel caused by the narrow space. If a diver was to get caught and carried out to sea, it would be for short distance. A diver who finds himself being carried off should not fight to swim against the current, since this would be a hopeless waste of energy. He should swim parallel to the beach, or across the current, until he gets out of the rip or the current disperses. Then he can easily make his way to the beach without having to fight against the current's force.

Whenever planning a dive in an area that has a strong current, it is best to dive at Slack Tide. Slack Tide simply means that for a short time there is little or no current. Slack occurs in the time lapse when the tide is changing from incoming to outgoing, or from outgoing to incoming. Slack Tide can last from five minutes to two hours, but will usually last for about a half-hour at most of Long Island's sites.

The best dives are usually done at High Slack because the incoming flooding tide has just brought in clean ocean water. During Low Slack, visibility is usually not as good due to the outgoing, Ebbing Tide, which brings out mud and debris from the inland waterways.

With the above information in mind, divers should refer to tide tables when planning their dives. Tide tables can be found in most fishing stores or in the daily paper. Make sure the table used is for the correct area since Slack Tide at one location will not occur at the same time as another.

Keep in mind that this is only a brief explanation of tides and currents. For more information, refer to an advanced dive manual, or participate in an advanced diver-training course. Remember: plan your dive and dive your plan.

TREASURE HUNTING

For anyone that likes to hunt for artifacts I would highly recommend an underwater metal detector. With a metal detector divers can find anything from buried brass and coins to lost jewelry. The other advantage is that any popular swim beach now becomes a great beach diving location. Even if the site offers little to attract divers. For example, a beach could have nothing but a barren sandy bottom with little marine life. However, buried beneath that sand could be old coins and gold rings. Divers also have an advantage over most treasure hunters who only wade chest deep into the water. Divers can, of course, swim out to the most lucrative spots, in water too deep to stand.

Photo by Jozef Koppelman

The *Atlantic Beach Bridge*. Photo by Daniel Berg

ATLANTIC BEACH BRIDGE

DIRECTIONS: (Atlantic Beach, Nassau County)

Take Sunrise Highway into the town of Lynbrook; turn south onto Broadway and continue. Broadway will change into Empire Avenue. Drive south, cross over Seagrit Boulevard and turn left on Seagrit Avenue. Then turn right on Beach 6th Street and take it to the end. Parking is usually not a problem.

CONDITIONS:

First let me say that this site is much more enjoyable and safer if a boat is used, instead of attempting the swim from shore. Although I would not recommend it, I have seen divers successfully reach the bridge from shore, so I feel obligated to inform you of the dive conditions and possibilities. By entering the water on the northwest side of the bridge towards the end of an incoming tide, divers can drift on the surface towards the bridge. When attempting this, stay close to shore and out of the channel. If timed correctly, divers can spear fish during slack tide and then at the first sign of an out going current, ride with the current back to their entry point. Another possibility is to park on the northeast side of the bridge, on Bannister Creek and catch the end of the outgoing tide to get to the bridge. Again, remember to stay close to the bulkhead. Dive the bridge during slack and then catch a ride back on the beginning of the incoming tide. Be sure to be on the surface, and close to the north side bulk heading when the current turns. Although this sounds easy, it is not. This area is heavily trafficked with boats and the current is extremely strong. Any miscalculation will conclude with divers, at the very least, having a long walk back.

Diving the bridge itself can be very rewarding. In fact, it is one of the best black fish spearing areas around. The best location is on the south side. Boats can tie up to her pilings and divers can descend to stalk their prey. Diving here should only be done at slack tide. When the tide is in the midst of running it is much too strong to swim against.

ATLANTIC BEACH OLD BRIDGE

DIRECTIONS: (Atlantic Beach, Nassau County)

Take Sunrise Highway into the town of Lynbrook; turn south onto Broadway and continue. Broadway will change into Empire Avenue. Drive south, cross over Seagrit Boulevard and turn left on Seagrit Avenue. Then turn right on Beach 6th Street and take it to the end. Parking is usually not a problem.

CONDITIONS:

About 50 feet east of the *Atlantic Beach Bridge* lie the remains of its predecessor. All that is left on the bottom is a long narrow group of rocks, concrete and pilings. For years, the location was easily spotted by looking for the remaining concrete structure in the otherwise wood bulkhead on either side of Reynolds Channel. Unfortunately, it is no longer easy to find as the concrete is now covered with new wood bulk-heading. The location will be found approximately 50 feet east of the new bridge. Diving the *Old Bridge* can be very rewarding. Not only is this area good for spear fishing and finding an occasional lobster, but divers will usually find a good assortment and variety of lost boat anchors.

I would strongly recommend that divers use a boat and anchor directly into the debris. Due to the debris on this site, anchors get caught and cannot be pulled out by their boat owners. However, divers unlike fishermen have the advantage of pulling their anchor after a dive is complete. I also would suggest only diving this area at slack tide and using a tether line to find the way back to the boat's anchor. As is the case with the *Atlantic Beach Bridge,* I have on occasion seen divers swim here from the beach. They follow the same directions as for the *Atlantic Beach Bridge,* coming from Beach 6th Street, but drift past the new bridge until the concrete debris is spotted on the bottom. The divers then descend and search through the debris. As the current starts its' way out divers should be on the surface on the north side close to the bulkhead. Staying close to the bulkhead while on the surface reduces the chance of being hit by one of the many pleasure craft that speed through the area. Another method used by divers to reach the bridge is to park on the northeast side on Bannister Creek, and drift with the end of the outgoing tide towards the bridge. Again, stay close to the bulkhead on the north side of Reynolds Channel. Dive the bridge during slack and then catch a ride back to your entry point at the beginning of the incoming tide. Be sure to be on the surface and close to the north side bulk heading when the current turns.

ATLANTIC BEACH JETTY

DIRECTIONS: **(Atlantic Beach, Nassau County)**

> *Note:* *This location is not accessible by car. The only way to dive this site is by boat.*

> *Note 2:* *In recent years the west side of this jetty has filled in with sand and is now very shallow. Diving may still be possible on the east side or out by the tip.*

CONDITIONS:

By boat, it is best to approach the *Atlantic Beach Jetty* on the inlet or west side. When diving this site, we have always dropped divers off at the southern-most end, or tip of the jetty. After covering the jetty's side, divers can explore the submerged jetty stones that can be found out past the tip. Black fish, striped bass, bregalls, starfish, crabs and lobster are all quite common here, because

The *Atlantic Beach Jetty*. Photo by Daniel Berg

only a few divers visit these submerged stones. After a predetermined amount of time, the divers would make their way back to the jetty's tip, where the boat would pick them up. Obviously not only a boat, but also a boat tender is needed.

Weather is also a very important factor when planning a dive here, as it will affect the wave action, and a flat, calm sea is preferable. All divers also should be aware of the strong current in Atlantic Beach Inlet.

The *Atlantic Beach Jetty* is not one of the best beach sites available to divers on Long Island, but the jetty along with the submerged rocks out by the point should definitely be visited by those experienced enough and those with the means of getting there.

BANNISTER CREEK BARGE

DIRECTIONS: **(Atlantic Beach, Nassau County)**

Take Sunrise Highway into the town of Lynbrook; turn south onto Broadway and continue. Broadway will change into Empire Avenue. Drive south. Turn left onto Seagrit Boulevard then before going over the Atlantic Beach Bridge turn onto the dirt lot on the east side. Parking here is usually not a problem.

> *Note: It is recommended to use a small boat or raft while crossing Bannister Creek.*

> *Note2: This entire cove was filled with sand during the powerful Nor'easter of 1992. The Bannister Creek Barge is now completely covered. I have left the listing in case Mother Nature decides to uncover the area in the near future.*

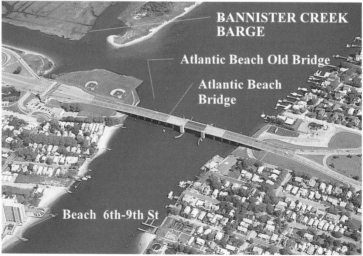

BANNISTER CREEK BARGE

Atlantic Beach Old Bridge

Atlantic Beach Bridge

Beach 6th-9th St

Photo by Daniel Berg

CONDITIONS:

The *Bannister Creek Barge*, rumored to be an old abandoned fire works barge, is located at the mouth of a side creek on the east side on Bannister Creek. The *Barge* is only partially submerged and can be easily located. The only down side or hazard to diving this site is the boat traffic when crossing Bannister Creek. Because the crossing is usually done close to the mouth, near Reynolds Channel, boats have very little time after turning into the creek to see and avoid divers. This is why it is highly recommended to use a small boat to cross this creek. Once at the barge, divers will find an intact wood barge sitting on a sand and silt bottom. The Barge rests on a 30-degree angle. Divers do not have to be concerned with currents in this side creek but should schedule their dive around high tide to assure the greatest possible visibility.

Penetration into the barge is possible through a square deck hatch on the west side of its' deck. Once inside divers will find a maze of cross beams along with a lot of silt. I have only been inside this barge a few times and there was truly nothing inside worth seeing. The only aquatic life thriving here were the largest bay eels I have ever seen. The exterior of the barge is covered with growth and is a good place to take macro photographs.

BAYVILLE BARGE AND SUB

DIRECTIONS: (Bayville, Nassau County)

Take the Long Island Expressway to Exit 41 North, which is 106, 107. When 106 & 107 split, bear right and stay on 106. Follow this all the way down past Northern Boulevard, and make a left on Berry Hill Road to the end. Make a left on Shore Drive to the end, then a right on Bayville Avenue. A few blocks up on the left is Greenwich Avenue. Both wrecks are located directly off this beach, but parking must be found elsewhere.

Bayville Barge & Sub are located just offshore of Greenwich Avenue. Photo by Dan Berg.

Bayville Barge

The author spearfishing at night on the *Bayville Barge*. Photo by Jozef Koppelman.

CONDITIONS:

This area is one of the best dive sites on Long Island. Water ranges from 15 to 25 feet on the barge and a little shallower on the sub. Visibility always seems to be good, and if the wind, weather and tide are right this area can be fishbowl clear.

To locate the barge, start at the water's edge directly in front of the pilings located on the east side of Greenwich Avenue, and swim out on a 330 degree compass course. It takes the average diver about 40 to 50 kick cycles to reach the wreck. The barge is home to huge black fish, striped bass, crabs, loads of small lobsters, and even an occasional two-pounder.

The sub, which lies slightly east in shallower water, is said to be a World War I, British-made, two-man reconnaissance sub. Whatever it was, the sub was put on this spot to act as a breakwater, and protect the beach from eroding. Rocks used in the breakwater's construction still cover most of the broken-up wreck. The only recognizable piece is a stabilizer fin that can be found on the northeast end of the small wreck. Car tires also can be found scattered in the sand around both wrecks. They usually provide a home to an easy to catch lobster.

Although this is a great dive site, parking and water access can be a real hassle. Divers can't blame anyone but themselves for the problems related to parking at this site. It seems that over the years local residents have become sick of being awakened at off hours and picking up garbage after a few bad apple divers.

Last I heard, the town of Bayville was going as far as thinking about banning water access to divers. What I have always done was to be very quiet and polite if anything was said. Also, patronizing the local waterfront restaurants is not only a good idea, but they serve great food.

Bayville is definitely one of my favorite beach dives. The site offers two wrecks within swimming distance, a fantastic array of aquatic life and, as I mentioned before, good waterfront restaurants. The *Bayville Barge* is also one of the most productive black fish spots on Long Island. Spearfishing here during the day can be very rewarding but the real secret is to go at night. The big black fish come in after dusk to sleep on the barge. All you have to do is swim around the barge with a light until you spot a big fish, usually nestled between some wreckage. A simple way of judging size is by looking at the color of a black fishes head. The fish with a white head is usually eight to twelve pounds. Since it is not very sporting to catch sleeping fish, we have always limited our take to only one or two big fish per diver.

The author and Bill Campbell with blackfish taken while night diving on the *Bayville Barge*. Photo by Steve Jonassen.

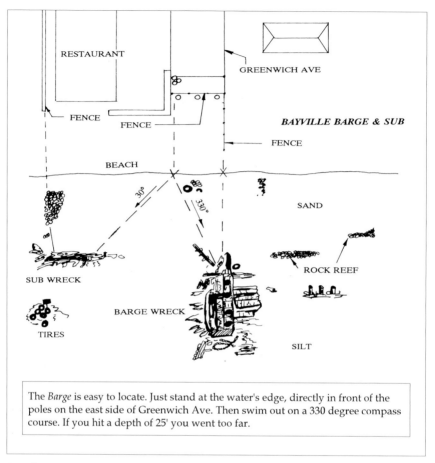

RESTAURANT

GREENWICH AVE

FENCE

FENCE

BAYVILLE BARGE & SUB

FENCE

BEACH

30°

330°

SAND

SUB WRECK

ROCK REEF

TIRES

BARGE WRECK

SILT

The *Barge* is easy to locate. Just stand at the water's edge, directly in front of the poles on the east side of Greenwich Ave. Then swim out on a 330 degree compass course. If you hit a depth of 25' you went too far.

Bayville Barge and Sub area sketch by Dan Berg.

BAYVILLE BEACH

DIRECTIONS: (Bayville, Nassau County)

Take the Long Island Expressway to Exit 41 North, which is 106, 107. When 106 & 107 split, bear right and stay on 106. Follow this all the way down past Northern Boulevard, and make a left on Berry Hill Road to the end. Make a left on Shore Drive to the end, then a left on Bayville Avenue. A few blocks up on the right is Bayville Town Beach.

CONDITIONS:

Diving here is only permitted off-season when the beach is closed to swimmers.

18

Diver Mike McMeekin from Treasures Unlimited enters the water with metal detector in hand.
Left: Four gold rings, a gold chain and several pieces of silver. Treasure from one very productive dive. Photos by Dan Berg

Divers must note that watercraft like jet skis and sailboats utilize the same area so a dive flag is mandatory. This site has easy parking a short walk to the beach and a clean sand bottom, which slopes off nicely to around 10-15 feet. Mike McMeekin and I started diving here a few years back. By using underwater metal detectors we started to recover all sorts of old coins. We found walking liberty half-dollars, buffalo nickels, mercury dimes, etc. After digging several hundred coins and then several hundred fishing sinkers we started to hit gold. For every several dives we did, we would each would come out of the water with a hand full of silver coins and one gold ring. Don't let anyone fool you, it was hard work. We dug holes for nearly two hours on each dive. On one dive both Mike and I each had five gold rings plus an assortment of silver rings and silver coins. Unfortunately, after a storm the most productive area filled in with sand and our treasure hunting dried up. Now occasionally we each return waiting for Mother Nature to uncover a new pocket of hidden treasure.

For scuba divers this site offers little more than covenant parking and sometimes crystal clear visibility. However, for those who use metal detectors it can be very productive.

Photo byRandi Eisen

BEACH 6th-9th STREET

DIRECTIONS: **(Far Rockaway, Nassau County)**

Take Sunrise Highway into the town of Lynbrook; turn south onto Broadway and continue. Broadway will change into Empire Avenue. Drive south, cross over Seagrit Boulevard and turn left on Seagrit Avenue. Then turn right on *Beach 8th Street* and take it to the end. Parking is usually not a problem, and at worst there will be a short walk. Please note that parking and water access can also be found on *Beach 6th* and *Beach 9th Street*.

CONDITIONS:

This site is now privately owned and operated. A small fee will be charged for parking but the owners provide fenced in and guarded parking, showers, rinse tanks, and rest rooms. Free access to the area is still available on *Beach 6th*. Water entry is easy at *Beach 8th & 9th Street.* Just walk across the beach and jump in. There are two or three small jetties jutting out from the beach. I usually enter the water and swim along the jetty in front of *Beach 8th Street.* The depth drops off very quickly to about 25 feet, only 30 feet off the beach. There are a few rock piles where blackfish and an occasional sand shark, or striped bass can be seen. According to Peter Nawrocky, a local underwater photographer and instructor, this site is excellent for macro photography. He reports visibility to be as good as 30 feet on good days.

Keep in mind that you are right in the Atlantic Beach Inlet, and the current can be quite strong if you swim out too far. Most of the fish stay close to the jetties, and I recommend that divers do the same. This spot is also used for fishing, so bring a sharp dive knife, as lost monofilament line can cause snags.

According to Captain Steve Bielenda, a local diving instructor, there is a submerged jetty a little bit west of *Beach 8th Street* just off *Beach 9th Street*. This area is a little less known, and therefore should be a more lucrative hunting ground for divers in search of lobsters.

My friend, Mike McMeekin, told me that once while diving here about 20 years ago, he spotted a shiny object lying amongst the mussels off a jetty slightly east of Beach 8th Street. The object turned out to be a beautiful antique gold ring with a sapphire and two diamonds. We are not sure how the ring got here, but I am convinced that hundreds of divers swam right over it before Mike's keen eyes found the prize.

BEACH 59th STREET WRECK

DIRECTIONS: (Far Rockaway, Queens)

Take the Southern State Parkway to Exit 19 South, which is Peninsula Boulevard. Drive south on Peninsula to Rockaway Turnpike and turn left. Turn right on Burnside Ave, and take Burnside to Beach Channel Drive and continue to head west. The wreck is located at the base of Summerville Basin on the bay side of 59th street. Parking is not currently available to the public and special arrangements would have to be made. As a side note, I would like to forewarn anyone who visits this area. This neighborhood is, to say the least, not the best. One of our biggest concerns when diving here was whether or not our car would be stolen while we were underwater.

CONDITIONS:

On the bay side of Far Rockaway just off 59th Steet is the remains of an 80 foot long, luxury yacht. The wreck appears to have sunk at its' slip and now sits upright and intact on a silty bottom in 25 feet of water.

Sketch of the *Beach 59th Street Wreck*. By Daniel Berg.

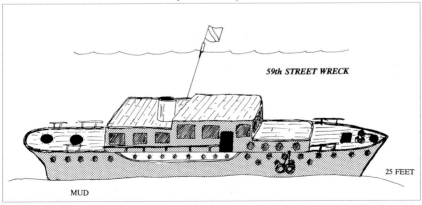

This wreck is big and penetration is possible. Remember that entering into any overhead environment should only be done by those who have the proper training, equipment and experience. In describing the wreck's layout I will start in the bow and work my way astern. Near the bow is a large square deck hatch; there is also a round one but that one only leads to a rope locker. By entering the square hatch and swimming astern you will pass a bathroom and a staircase on the port side. This corridor leads to the vessel's engine room where two diesels are located. The silt in this wreck is kicked up very easily so be careful. Instead of entering the engine room, the alternative is to head up the spiral staircase. These stairs lead to her main salon. To exit this room, swim to the far starboard corner. This area also can be reached by entering the doorway on the starboard side of her pilothouse. If divers enter this doorway and head forward the first left turn will lead into her pilothouse, the next room is the galley, and finally the large dining room. From the stern, the only recommended way into the wreck is through the door into the aft cabin. This is a large room with a silt-covered floor. In the forward port corner is another spiral staircase that leads down to the sleeping quarters. At the bottom of the stairs divers will find a corridor that leads aft, but be careful, as this corridor is very collapsed.

Darryl Steinhauser of Dive, Inc. first brought me to this wreck back in 1988. The wreck was located behind an old abandoned, burnt down boat yard. On my first dive here I was lucky enough to recover a brass porthole. Over the next two years we would dive this wreck whenever it was too rough to get offshore. We have retrieved more than twenty portholes of three different sizes, and an assortment of cage lamps, fittings, horns and china. Steve Jonassen found one of the easiest portholes recovered. He found it inside a cabinet drawer, apparently set aside as a spare part. Many of the portholes were found by swimming around the outside of the wreck until a porthole with glass was spotted. Then one diver would shine his light through the glass and the other would go inside to look for the light beam. By using this method we located several portholes that would have otherwise been missed. Some were inside closets; some behind shelves and one was located behind a large electrical fuse box.

The whole area around the wreck is also very productive. In fact, while navigating from shore to the wreck we found at least ten other smaller cabin cruiser wrecks. In 1991, the old boat yard was sold and a new boat yard was built. Many of the smaller wrecks were raised and new pilings and floating docks were installed. Amazingly, the *59th Street Wreck* remained untouched. The wreck is under the west side floating dock about 100 feet offshore. Unfortunately, I do not believe the owners of the new boat yard would appreciate divers swimming under their docks, but who knows, maybe in the winter when all the boats are pulled they might give permission.

The author with a large four dog brass porthole.
Photo by Jozef Koppelman

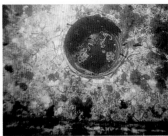

Diver Bill Campbell found and recovered this porthole from the *Beach 59th Street Wreck*. Photos by Daniel Berg

The author with one of the medium size portholes from the wreck. Photo by Rick Schwarz.

Captain Rick Schwarz with an engine room porthole. Photo by Daniel Berg

The authors charter dive boat anchored over *Black Banks.* Photo by Daniel Berg

Phil Senk with two Blackfish taken at *Black Banks.* Photo by Daniel Berg

BLACK BANKS

DIRECTIONS: (Nassau County)

NOTE: *This location is not accessible by car. The only way to dive this site is by boat.*

CONDITIONS:

Black Banks is located on the north side of Reynolds Channel just east of the Wantagh Pkwy, Bridge. Although only accessible by boat this is one of the best inshore dives in the area. When timed correctly so that divers are in the water at high slack it's not uncommon to have over 20' visibility. There are several small wrecks, which are attached by a steel cable, for easy navigation. This is a great spot for spear fishing. Schools of large blackfish can be found not only along the steep clay walls but also around each wreck. Due to a very strong current, divers should note that diving here should only be done during slack water. Of course, high slack, which is usually about two hours after Jones Inlet provides the best chance of enhanced visibility.

CAUMSETT STATE PARK

DIRECTIONS: (Lloyd Neck, Suffolk County)

Take the Long Island Expressway to Exit 49 North. Take Route 110 to Route 25A and turn left. Drive west to West Neck Road and turn right. Drive north on West Neck Road to the park entrance.

Topside photos
by Pete Nawrocky

Photo by Randi Eisen

CONDITIONS:

Diving *Caumsett State Park* requires a special permit. The permits are limited and are given out on a first-come, first-serve basis from the Parks Department at Belmont Lake State Park. The permit is issued per car, so I suggest squeezing as many divers as you can into one vehicle. This site was first opened to diving after L.I.D.A. (Long Island Diving Association) obtained permission from the Parks Department a few years back.

Caumsett Park is typical of many north shore dive sites. Divers will find easy beach access, a sand bottom, and if they swim east for about 250 yards, some scattered rocks. Depth ranges from about four to 15 feet, and there is a fair amount of marine life, especially seaweed. This site happens to be especially good for practicing underwater navigation. Others simply enjoy this site for an early season tune-up dive. According to Janice Raber, the park recently put in steps going from the parking lot down to the beach. This addition makes it even easier for beach divers to access the site.

CEDAR BEACH & JETTIES

DIRECTIONS: (Mount Sinai, Suffolk County)

Take the Long Island Expressway to Exit 63 North, Patchogue Road. Drive north to the end and make a right. Bear left on Echo Avenue; then make a left onto Pipe Stave Hollow Road. Take this to the end and make a left on Harbor Beach Road to the end. You will enter a large parking lot; drive through to a

Cedar Beach and Jetties

Aerial photo of *Cedar Beach and Jetties*. Photo courtesy Hank Garvin

small dirt parking lot on the right, or you can continue to the turn around, drop off your dive gear, then park.

CONDITIONS:

Diving can be done directly off the beach where clear calm water can usually be found. This is a good site for basic divers to experience aquatic life, such as fluke, flounder, and spider crabs. An occasional lobster can be found living in one of the car tires found off the beach.

The other options for the more experienced divers are either of the two jetties. The only diving found on the east jetty is out by the point. Here, there are many rocks to search between for lobsters. I think all divers would enjoy this jetty, but the west jetty is by far the better of the two. On it are an abundant supply of lobsters, plus the remains of at least two small wrecks. Both were sunk during the hurricane of 1985. Although not too much wreckage will be found, divers will still see debris scattered in and amongst the rocks on the west side of the west jetty. A good deal of brass artifacts from these wrecks can still be recovered.

Always be cautious when swimming to the west jetty, as the current can be very strong through this inlet. When possible I prefer to use an underwater propulsion unit.

Back in 1986, after a winter storm, Bill Campbell and I noticed a sailboat had drifted onto the west jetty's rocks. The next day when Bill and I were ready to dive it, the wreck was gone. After we had navigated across the inlet, the only trace we found was red paint and some scattered wreckage on the east side of the west jetty. The current must have carried the main wreck away. On the same dive, Bill and I took a look on the west side of the west jetty and found another wreck. This one was a twin-engine cabin cruiser. This wreck was scattered amongst the jetty's rocks and half buried in the sand next to the jetty.

During one dive here I noticed a four-wheel-drive vehicle on the inlet's west side. Finding access on the west side, as these four-wheel-drive vehicles have done, would eliminate the grueling swim across the inlet. Divers should always fly a dive flag here and stay aware of the heavy boat traffic.

CENTER ISLAND BEACH

DIRECTIONS: (Center Island, Nassau County)

Take the Long Island Expressway to Exit 41 North, Route 106, 107. When 106 and 107 split, bear right and stay on 106. Follow this all the way up past Northern Boulevard and make a left turn on Berry Hill Road to the end. Make a left on Shore Drive to the end, then a right on Bayville Avenue. Stay on Bayville Avenue until you come to a small police station. On your right side will be the bay and on your left side will be the sound. This is where the dive site is. Drop off your dive gear, turn around and drive to the beach parking lot that is located on the bay side.

This Diamond ring was recovered by Mike McMeekin while metal detecting around *Center Island Beach.*
Photo by Dan Berg

Photo courtesy Pete Nawrocky.

Center Island Beach. Photo by Daniel berg

27

CONDITIONS:

On the east end of *Center Island Beach* is a small rock jetty, and further east is a cement wall. Divers should plan to swim along this wall out to the point. This is where the best diving can be done. Some huge boulders can be seen from the surface, and many more are scattered just below. Lobsters can usually be found here. Most of the rocks, where the lobsters are to be found, are only a short swim apart, so after the first couple of dives here you will learn the best locations, and should certainly be able to catch the limit of bugs (lobsters).

The only thing I found annoying about this site was the shallow slope to the beach. It seemed like I had to walk and swim forever before I could find water over five feet deep. After the dive, the swim in to shore was even worse due to a mild outgoing current.

Taking everything into account, *Center Island Beach* is a good dive. If it wasn't for the long swim, I'm sure *Center Island* would be a much more popular dive site.

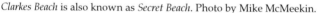

CLARKES BEACH

DIRECTIONS: (Southold, Suffolk County)

Take the Long Island Expressway to Exit 73 East. This will be Old Country Road. Take Old Country Road until it turns into Main Road. This takes you

Clarkes Beach is also known as *Secret Beach.* Photo by Mike McMeekin.

into Southold where you will make a left onto Young's Avenue. From Young's make a right onto Middle Road. You will see water on your left side. You also will see a Greenport sign on the right side of the road, which will be 1.5 miles from the turn off. About a half mile before the turn off there will be a motel on the left hand side. When you come to a dirt road on the left, turn left and follow it to the water.

CONDITIONS:

This north shore dive site is also known to some as *Secret Beach*. Diving can be quite good here due to a clean sandy bottom. Some scattered large rocks are homes for all types of marine life. Depth of water ranges from 15 to 25 feet, and divers will feel a mild tidal flow, mostly when swimming on the surface.

This site is often used by diving instructors for open water training because of the commonly good visibility, lack of strong current and parking availability. In fact, during some spring weekends, this place is anything but a secret beach, since there can be anywhere from ten to over 100 divers participating in open water dive training.

H.M.S. CULLODEN

DIRECTIONS: **(Montauk, Suffolk County)**

Take Southern State Parkway to Exit 44 East, Sunrise Highway. Stay on Sunrise to Montauk Highway. Continue on Montauk Highway past the town of

H.M.S. Culloden was commissioned on May 18th, 1776.

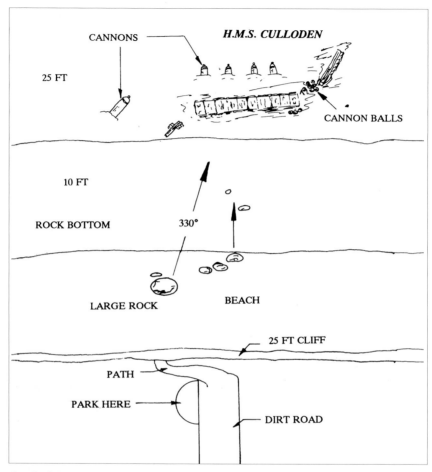

Sketch of the *Culloden* wreck site by Daniel Berg.

Montauk, and make a left turn onto Edgemere Street, which will turn into West Lake Drive. Follow this to the end and turn left onto Soundview Drive. Take Soundview until it turns into a dirt road. At this point you will have to continue straight ahead for .2 miles. Turn right onto another dirt road (no name) and continue to the end.

Note: The publisher offers a 1/2 hour VHS video documentary on the Culloden.

CONDITIONS:

The *H.M.S. Culloden* was a 170-foot by 47 foot, 74-gun English frigate, commissioned on May 18th, 1776. The Culloden was armed with twenty-eight 32-pounders, twenty-eight 18-pounders and eighteen 9-pound cannons.

On January 22, 1781, the *Culloden* under the command of Captain Balfour, along with the vessels America and the Bedford waited in Block Island Sound

Above: The author uses a propulsion unit to blast away sand uncovering on of the *Culloden's* cannons. Photo by Jozef Koppelman.
Left: Aerial photograph of *Culloden Wreck* site. Photo by Dan Berg.

for several French warships that were reportedly about to run the British blockade. The next night brought not the expected French warships, but a powerful gale. The three British ships headed for the open sea to ride out the storm. The *Culloden*, with Third Lieutenant, John Cannon at watch, was following Bedford's lights. At around 12:30 am the Bedford came about. Captain Balfour of the *Culloden* decided to maintain course, but ordered a sounding to be taken every half hour. At 4:00 am Long Island's coastline loomed directly in front of the *Culloden.* Before any action could be taken the ship went aground. After the storm had ended every possible effort was made to re-float the *Culloden* but nothing could be done. The *Culloden* had been severely damaged. Captain Balfour ordered that everything valuable be transferred to shore. Later, he sent a boat to Gardiner's Island to report the disaster. The vessel, William and the Brig, Adventure were sent to salvage the *Culloden's* cannons, gun carriages and anchors. The only guns left aboard were her obsolete 32-pound iron cannons, but even these were spiked so they would not be salvaged and put to use by the French or Americans. After salvaging was complete the *Culloden* was set afire and burned to the water line. This was done so the vessel would be of no use in the American Revolution.

In July of 1781, despite British efforts to render the guns useless, Joseph Woodbridge of Groton, Connecticut, salvaged 16 of the *Culloden's* 32-pound

Culloden

cannons and offered them to General George Washington.

Today, this once proud "Ship of the Line" rests in about 20 feet of water just off Culloden Point in Montauk. The wreckage lies on a compass course of 330 degrees from the big rock on the beach. The wreck lies only about 150 feet offshore. If you get deeper than about 25 feet, you have passed her. Once the wreck is located, divers will note that not too much wreckage remains exposed. A testimony to the constant pounding of winter storms are the wreck's scattered remains which have been buried beneath the ever-changing sand bottom. Just north of her wreckage, about ten feet from the nearest visible wood plank, are four of her cannons. The cannons all face towards shore and are almost always completely covered with sand. Many divers have passed right over them, thinking they were only rocks. Inshore from her cannons and on the eastern most edge of the wreck divers can still see cannon balls. In 1992, Mike McMeekin and I found a 5th cannon on the site. This cannon is inshore and west of the main group. Again, most of the wreck is covered in sand so fanning will be necessary to recognize the cannons.

A few years back this wreck was salvaged, but divers who are lucky enough to dive here should keep an eye out for some of the remains. The cannons are rumored to weigh over 10,000 pounds and have a diameter similar to a large garbage can. The *Culloden* is the only local shipwreck on the National Register of Historic Shipwrecks and as such is a protected site. Divers should take nothing but photographs and leave nothing but bubbles when exploring this historic area.

Recently, there has been talk about making the *Culloden* an underwater park. The plan, as recently stated in a NEW YORK OUTDOORS magazine article, is to build a museum on Culloden Point, and set up guided underwater tours. At this point I don't know the exact plans or implications to divers, but I am, to say the least, a little skeptical. I'm hoping that they continue to allow divers unrestricted access to the wreck without charging a fee. Recently, I was denied permission to even look at the one *Culloden* cannon on exhibit at the East Hampton Town Marine Museum. Although this is supposedly a public museum, once they found out that I was a diver and wanted to photograph the artifact, the doors were slammed shut. Obviously, this museum does not want to encourage recreational diving at the site. Unfortunately, I fear the same type of discrimination may take place with the planned underwater park. However, I do feel that divers, as long as diving access remained unchanged, would strongly support a *Culloden Museum* located on *Culloden Shores.* When planning for the underwater park, it would be nice if local authorities took into consideration the rights and needs of divers, who are the only group of citizens currently enjoying the *Culloden* wreck.

According to Janice Raber, the town of East Hampton recently purchased the *Culloden Property*. The property is now a public park.

CUPSOQUE BEACH COUNTY PARK

DIRECTIONS: (West Hampton , Suffolk County)

From the village of West Hampton, go south on Jessup Lane and cross the bridge. Turn right onto Dune Road. Take Dune Road to the end.

CONDITIONS:

Suffolk County recently opened up many of its parks to scuba divers. This beach dive on the back-bay side of the inlet should be planned for slack tide. Depth is approximately 12 feet.

DEMOCRAT POINT

DIRECTIONS: (Fire Island, Suffolk County)

NOTE: This location is not accessible by car. The only way to dive this site is by boat.

CONDITIONS:

Democrat Point, located on the east side of Fire Island Inlet, happens to be not one, but two fantastic dive sites. Because divers can only get to these sites by boat, the number of divers has always been limited.

Democrat Point is located on the east side of Fire Island inlet. Photo by Daniel Berg

Photo by Pete Nawrocky

33

Democrat Point/Derelict Bay

The first site is located on the jetty, on the south side of *Democrat Point*. Divers should be aware of the currents that sweep through Fire Island Inlet, plus watch the weather. I know I would not want to try diving the jetty when the surf was up. Once here, divers will find themselves on a clean sand bottom with the jetty acting like a fish haven. Divers will not only find lobsters, black fish, striped bass, fluke, flounder, crabs and mussels, but a good amount of monofilament line, since this is also a popular fishing site. Due to the current, I would suggest diving only be done here at slack tide. Depth ranges from ten to about 20 feet.

The second location is situated on the north side. Divers will find a small area sheltered from most tidal currents, with large submerged rocks, and a hole that drops to about 40 feet at high tide. This hole has the nickname, *Bottle Hole*, because it acts as a catch basin for discarded bottles, which, until caught here, drift with the current along the inlet's sandy bottom.

For anyone with a boat, especially if it's located near Fire Island Inlet, I would definitely recommend diving the north side. I believe that all will enjoy the abundant amount and variety of marine life.

DERELICT BAY

DIRECTIONS: (Suffolk County)

NOTE: This location is not accessible by car. The only way to dive this site is by boat.

CONDITIONS:

Derelict Bay is located just off Reynolds Channel, half way between Jones Inlet and Fire Island Inlet. The bay is almost directly across from East Fox Creek. Back in 1992, Hank Garvin and I were flying over Long Island in a little single engine Cessna, when I spotted a shipwreck. The wreck was located in a small cove just west of Captree Boat Basin. The wreck appeared to be about 45' long and was sitting awash on her starboard side in the middle of the bay.

One-week later, divers Billy Campbell, Mike McMeekin, Donovan Berg and I were heading offshore for a late October dive. Bad weather cancelled our offshore plans so we decided to check out the little wreck in the bay. After cruising east we slowly inched our way closer to find not one wreck but about a dozen small wrecks scattered on shore and a few wrecks sticking through the surface. As we approached the 45' wreck it seemed a little strange. Although, the wreck was hard aground, my depth recorder still showed over 20 feet of water under our boat. Later we learned that this wreck was actually sitting on top of a sunken barge.

34

Donovan Berg, Bill Campbell and Mike McMeekin with portholes from *Derelict Bay*. Photo by Daniel Berg

The author with small brass porthole.
Photo by Mike McMeekin

Mike McMeekin holds a bronze propeller he recovered. Photo by Dan Berg

Photo by Denise Berg

Derelict Bay

I was the first to suit up and snorkel over to the wreck. There was no sense in all of us getting wet if there were no artifacts, especially since we had been planning on an offshore dive and were set up with double tanks. As I circled the wreck and free dove down to her submerged starboard side I spotted the first brass porthole. Within a minute I found three more. The final count was seven. I returned to get my tanks and tools as Mike, Bill and Donovan were suiting up. Within a half hour all four of us were working furiously. In fact, it sounded more like a construction site than a scuba dive. There were two different size portholes on the wreck. I started working on one of the small ones mounted amidships. After about ten minutes the porthole was free. Mike also had a small porthole. We then moved to the bow, where Billy and Donovan seemed to be swinging their sledge hammers in rhythm. These portholes were not as easy. Mike and I squeezed inside through a hatch and assisted the guys with a crow bar. We were all now a little tired and headed back to the Wreck Valley.

After lunch, Donovan snorkeled to shore to check out the other small visible wrecks for brass. Billy would search the bays bottom for sunken boats. Mike and I figured the 45' wreck would have a nice size propeller and went back in with a hack saw to work on it. After another long working dive, Mike and I were able to get through the two-inch propeller shaft. Later, when we were all back aboard we had a total of seven brass portholes, three propellers, a Danford anchor and an assortment of brass fittings. I'm still not sure why all these wrecks are in the same bay but I was told that the Coast Guard uses this cove to dump derelict vessels. This explanation makes sense and also means that the area will be restocked with wrecks every few years.

As a side note, in 1999, Ed Slater and Aaron Hirsh returned to *Derelict Bay* and recovered a nice oval shaped brass porthole.

Photo by Dan Berg.

Capt. Dan and his
son Christopher
with propeller
recovered from the
Done Deal.
Photo by Rick Schwarz.

Every winter seals can be found in the area
of the *Done Deal.* . Photo by Daniel Berg

DONE DEAL

DIRECTIONS: (Nassau County)

NOTE: *Although this wreck rests less than 50 feet from shore. This location is not accessible by car. The only way to dive this site is by boat. GPS 40 36.130, 073 32.190. The publisher also offers a VHS video detailing our salvage of the Done Deal.*

CONDITIONS:

The *Done Deal* is a cabin cruiser, which had been abandoned on Jones Island, on the north side of Reynolds Channel, between Meadowbrook and Wantagh bridges. The wreck eventually drifted off the island and settled in 25 feet of water just west of Haunts Creek. Diver, Freddy Belise was the first diver to locate the wreck. He picked quite a bit of brass from her remains and by cleaning marine growth off her stern was able to read the name "*Done Deal*" . During the winter of 1996, we salvaged both of her bronze propellers, rudders and a teak swim platform. The wreck now sits upright, but mostly buried on a clean sand bottom. Divers will find a heavy current in the area so diving at slack tide is highly recommended.

The sand and gravel bottom plus offshore rock beds make *Duck Pond Point* a fantastic dive site. Photo by Daniel Berg.

DUCK POND POINT

DIRECTIONS: **(Southold, Suffolk County)**

Take the Long Island Expressway to Exit 73 East. This will be Old Country Road and will change into Route 25, Main Road. Continue east on 25 until you reach the town of Mattituck. Turn left on Wickhan Avenue; this will change into Middle Road. Make a left onto Depot Lane, which will lead into Duck Pond Road. Be sure to stay on Duck Pond Road (it curves right towards the end). Parking here is not the best, but space is usually available for one or two cars.

CONDITIONS:

Duck Pond Point is a fantastic dive site. The sand and gravel bottom, plus offshore rock beds make a great home to some decent size black fish, and a good amount of lobsters. Depth of water is about 15 feet, which, although shallow, is common for north shore sites. Divers who swim more than a couple of hundred yards offshore will find little more than a mud bottom. I would stay around the rocks and look for lobsters.

Divers can enter directly off the beach or take a short walk west to some large rocks, which is a good area for spear fishing. You can then casually swim back while searching for lobsters along the offshore rocks that run parallel to shore.

This site also should be tried as a night dive. The potential of finding lobsters, which are nocturnal feeders, or seeing an occasional squid will be the reward enjoyed by those who dive at night.

Aerial photograph of *Dutch Springs*.
Photo courtesy Pete Nawrocky.

Photo by Pete Nawrocky

DUTCH SPRINGS

DIRECTIONS: (Bethlehem, PA)

Note: Although not located on Long Island, I decided to include this site because so many local shops utilize Dutch Springs for open water training.

From the George Washington Bridge take I-95 South to I-78 West. Or take the Verrazano Bridge to I-278 west to I-95 North to I-78 West. Stay on

I-78 West to Rt. 22 (Exit 3 - last exit in NJ) to Rt. 191 North. Take Rt. 191 to Hanoverville Road (approx. 1 mile north of Rt. 22); make a left, *Dutch Springs* is approximately 1 mile on left. For additional information contact *Dutch Springs* at (610) 759-2270

CONDITIONS:

Note: The following text was provided by Dutch Springs and taken from an article written by Pete Nawrocky.

Dutch Springs is a 47-acre lake located just two hours from the New York border. Originally, this area was farmland and the lake did not exist. The National Portland Cement Company discovered a rich limestone deposit and purchased the farmland. The limestone was quarried out and as the excavation worked deeper into the ground the quarry began to flood. Pumps were used to remove the water. As the work continued a depth of 100 feet was reached.

Dutch Springs

Eventually, the narrowing profit margin caused the business to close. The pumps were shut off, the quarry flooded and became a lake.

Dutch Springs now offers unique diving opportunities to divers of varying levels. Quarry equipment can still be found on the bottom. One of the pump houses can be found at a depth of 70 feet. Other items have also been placed in the lake for divers. Currently a Cessna airplane (35'), fire truck (25'), a trolley (70'), school bus (55'), the Silver Comet (65') and a 80' long Sikorsky H-37 helicopter which is suspended off the bottom. *Dutch Springs* includes a dive site map with each admission, so finding the different items is easy.

In addition, a stocking program was established. Trout, bass, blue-gills, large gold fish, koi and cray fish are abundant in the lake.

It is possible to experience 30 feet of visibility but warm temperatures can trigger algae growth and drop visibility down to 15 feet. After the dive hot and cold showers and a heated changing area are available.

A crane lifts a trolley car to put it into *Dutch Springs*. The Trolley was already rigged with several large Sub-Salve lift bags. The Trolley was then floated into position and sunk. The Trolley is now just one of the many objects divers can explore in *Dutch Springs*. Photos by Daniel Berg

The published offers a half hour VHS video documentary film on *Dutch Springs.*

EATONS NECK OYSTER BARGE

DIRECTIONS: (Eatons Neck, Suffolk County)

Take the Long Island Expressway to Exit 51 North, Deer Park Avenue. Bear right at the fork on Deer Park Road East and take this to Jericho Turnpike and turn right. Then make the first left onto Elwood Road. Drive north on Elwood to Route 25, Forth Salonga Road. Make a left, then a quick right on Reservoir Avenue, and continue to drive north. Reservoir will change into Church Street, then into Ocean Avenue that you will follow to the end. Turn left on Eatons Neck Road; this will turn into Asharoken Avenue, and then back into Eatons Neck Road. (Be careful: the speed limit on Eatons Neck Road is 30 mph, and it is strictly enforced.) Make a right turn on Tudor Drive, then a right onto Birmingham. Birmingham will take you into a town beach. Go to the far end of the parking lot and park. The wreck is located on the bay side about a quarter mile down the beach.

Sketch of the *Eatons Neck Oyster Barge* area. Sketch by Daniel Berg

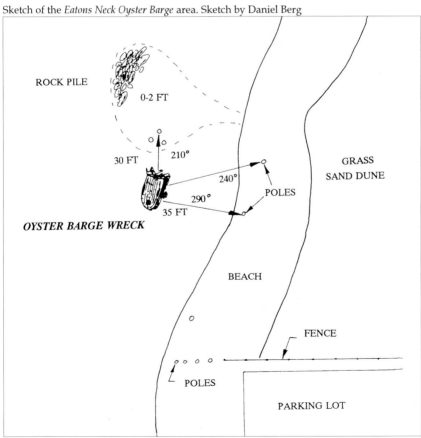

CONDITIONS:

The *Oyster Barge* rests on a sloping bottom where depth ranges from a mere five feet close to shore, to almost 40 feet at the wreck's deep end. The barge is mostly intact with one wall collapsed. The bottom is composed of muddy silt, which can, and usually does reduce visibility to zero when kicked up. When I was first brought to this site, I dove with a group of divers. The first two were the only ones to see the wreck while the rest of us literally had to feel our way around.

I would recommend that only small groups dive here at one time, with all divers making a conscious effort not to stir up the bottom. If kicking is kept to a minimum, and the wind and tide are right, I'm told divers can see all sorts of crabs, small invertebrates, mussels, oysters, and even mantis shrimp.

Spear fishermen can even enjoy this site by lying down near the edge of the barge on the top deck. Here they can enjoy better visibility by not kicking up the silt and can wait for passing black fish to swim within range.

A word of caution to all divers: Since this wreck is heavily fished and holds a good amount of monofilament line, a sharp knife should always be carried. Also, when visibility is zero, a diver could unknowingly swim inside the collapsed wall. Just remember that caution is always the key to a safe and enjoyable dive.

FORT POND BAY

DIRECTIONS: (Montauk, Suffolk County)

Take Southern State Parkway to Exit 44 East, Sunrise Highway. Stay on Sunrise to Montauk Highway and continue east into the town of Montauk. Turn left onto Second House Road and drive north to the water. Turn right onto Navy Road. Navy Road will end at a gate. This area is private property and permission is needed to park here. If you turn left onto Navy Road, you will end up in a condo development. This is also private property but I have been told that is possible to park just before the condo entrance.

CONDITIONS:

Fort Pond Bay is a good beginner beach dive, and is used quite often by dive shops conducting their open water diver training sessions. Divers can find all types of marine life along with quite a bit of seaweed. Visibility can be very good and, as always, high tide is the best time to plan your dive here.

Back in World War II *Fort Pond Bay* was used as a U.S. Navy Submarine Base. Because of this military presence, some interesting artifacts have been

42

Aerial photo of *Fort Pond Bay*. Photo by Daniel Berg

recovered in the area. Many divers walk or swim to the long pier in front of the condos. On and around the pier, divers have found everything from bullets to bottles, and I know of one diver who was lucky enough to recover a rifle.

GARVEYS POINT JETTY

DIRECTIONS: (Glen Cove, Nassau County)

Take the Long Island Expressway to Exit 39 North, Glen Cove Road. Take this to the end and turn left onto Glen Cove Avenue. Make the first right turn onto Charles Street. Go to the end and make a left on The Place road. Make the second left on McLoughlin Street and drive to the end.

CONDITIONS:

Getting to this site requires a little walking. Although I haven't tried, I don't believe diving would be permitted during the summer while the park is open. As with any beach site, use courtesy and don't leave garbage around for someone else to pick up. This will help to insure the accessibility of this site for future years.

The jetty is located to the east of McLoughlin Street. Access during the winter months is usually available through a gate on the east side of the street. Walk down the beach and begin your dive at the base of the jetty.

Garveys Point Jetty is located just east of McLoughlin Street Photo by Daniel Berg.

Right: The author holds a rectangular brass porthole. Photo by Rick Schwarz.

I have found the west side of the jetty to have good visibility while the east side is consistently murky. This is caused not only by divers, but also by any type of wave action.

During the day I was not very impressed with the amount of fish life, but I've been told that night dives can be quite rewarding. I was also informed that diving off the west tip of the jetty would put divers into a very lucrative bottling area. Be sure to have a dive flag, as it will not only help you avoid being cast upon by fishermen, but also will help to avoid a fine from the harbor patrol boat that frequently cruises the area.

In the winter of 1991, Rick Schwarz and I noticed some large wreckage with a square shaped hole up on the jetty. Before walking out to see what it was I jokingly said that it was a wreck and I called dibs on the porthole. Rick laughed, but as we slowly walked out over the ice-covered rocks we found a wreck smashed up onto the jetty. On one board sticking out of the water was a rectangular brass porthole. I didn't even have to get wet. Rick and I later spent over an hour in the near freezing water looking around the wreckage for another porthole. Although there should certainly be another one we never found it. The wreck can be found just about half way out on the west side.

GARVEYS POINT MOORING AREA

DIRECTIONS: (Glen Cove, Nassau County)

Take the Long Island Expressway to Exit 39 North, Glen Cove Road. Take this to the end where it changes names to Pratt Boulevard. Make a left on Glen Cove Avenue and the first right onto Charles Street. Take this to the end and make a left onto The Place Road, then make the second left onto McLoughlin Street. Drive to the end and park. Water access is obtained by walking through

Mike McMeekin, Ed Jeny and Louie Schiener with bottles recovered from *Garveys Point*. Photo by Dan Berg.

The author holds bottles recovered from *Garveys Point*. Photo by Mike McMeekin.

the wild life preserve. I have not had any problems in the past, but as usual, I recommend that divers go in small groups and use common courtesy.

Note: The Publisher also offers a VHS video documentary about bottle diving at Garveys Point.

CONDITIONS:

Walk down the dirt path, then along the beach to the first small jetty. Most diving is done to the west of this jetty due to the mud and silt that is found to the east. After swimming out a short distance, divers should find some large rocks that lie parallel to the beach. There are usually a few lobsters here, so be sure to take a look. As you proceed out, the bottom will change from sand to hard mud, and then finally to soft mud. Just stay off the bottom and try not to murk up the water. You will then be sure to find all types of bottles. Many of these bottles date back to the late 1800's.

There is also a small wreck in the area. We named this small cabin boat, *Perko,* because all the brass recovered from the wreck had the manufacturer's name, *Perko*, stamped on it. This site is also used as a mooring area, so boat traffic

45

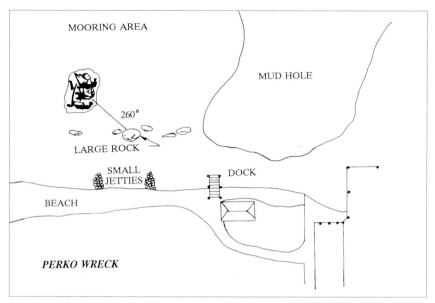

Sketch of the *Garveys Point Mooring Area* and *Perko wreck*. sketch by Daniel Berg.

should be expected in season. Each team of divers should tow a diver's flag. This is the only way a boat captain can be expected to know that you're in the water. I usually try to dive here off-season or at night when the traffic isn't as heavy.

Back in the spring of 1984, I was diving here for bottles with Rick Schwarz, Billy Campbell and Steve Jonassen. We had tied our dive flag off and had been swimming in search patterns looking for bottles. On this day I was the last one in the water. During the last ten minutes of the dive I heard a powerboat overhead. I navigated back to our dive flag and then swam into the beach. When I came ashore, I learned that a police boat had been following my bubbles. I was nowhere near our flag and the officer on board wanted to give me a ticket for diving without a flag. His only problem was that after following me for 15 minutes, when I exited the water I was holding a dive flag. His next move was out of pure spite, as he proceeded to write me a ticket for "Diving In A Mooring Area." Since that day I have never had another problem at the site, but please be aware of the possibilities and always stay close to your flag.

GREENPORT BRIDGE

DIRECTIONS: (Southold, Suffolk County)

The *Greenport Bridge* is located on Long Island's north fork between Hashamomuck Pond and Mill Creek. Take the L.I.E. to Exit 73, Old Country

Road. Drive east on Old Country into the town of Southold. Old Country will have changed into Main Road. The *Railroad Bridge* is located on the north side of the car bridge, .8 miles past Laurel Avenue. There is no good parking close to the bridge, but I was told that divers can access the spot either by a small boat, or with a short walk.

CONDITIONS:

The *Greenport Bridge*, or *Railroad Bridge*, as it is sometimes called, is a good dive for those who like to muck around looking for old bottles, or even dishes. Why bottles and china are found at this location is

Mike McMeekin holds bottles from the *Greenport Railroad Bridge.* Photo by Daniel Berg

unknown. The site was possibly once used as a dumping area. The bottom is mostly mud, so visibility is often poor. Even when visibility is good, the bottom gets mucked up easily. I would suggest that divers try to hover over the bottom, and when swimming, try to kick with their fins on a slight upward angle. There is a running current under the bridge that can either be avoided by diving during slack tide, or worked with by diving the small pond south of the bridge, and not directly under the trestle.

The rewards do sometimes justify the means. In this case, it's worth feeling your way around in zero visibility to reap the once plentiful supply of blob-top beer bottles dating back to the late 1800's.

GREENPORT JETTY

DIRECTIONS: (Southold, Suffolk County)

Take the Long Island Expressway east to Exit 73, Old Country Road. Drive east on Old Country Road, through the traffic circle, and make a left onto Northville Turnpike. Drive north to the end and turn right on Sound Avenue. Continue east. Sound Avenue will become Middle Road and then Main Road. Drive for .5 miles and turn right on Beach Road. Drive .3 miles and turn right on Bay Road. This will take you to the jetty, but not to any parking. Go back to Manhasset and drive south into Norman E. Klipp Marine Park, or public beach to park. In season, this parking lot is posted as open by permit only. I was told that non-residents would be charged for beach access.

CONDITIONS:

The *Greenport Jetty* is located on the south side of the north fork. This jetty has

Aerial photo of the *Greenport Jetty*. Photo by Daniel Berg.

Lobster on the *Greenport Jetty*. Photo by Jozef Koppelman.

to be one of the longest on Long Island, as it seems to go on forever. Visibility in the area is usually good, since the jetty is protected from northwest winds. Even winds from the south don't seem to disturb the bottom too much.

Divers exploring the jetty at night have reported seeing squid, mantis shrimp, sleeping black fish, clams, scallops, mussels and even a good supply of the ever popular lobster.

From the public beach, there is about a half-mile walk to the jetty, so I would only recommend this site to those who are used to this type of walk while carrying or wearing full dive gear.

HEMPSTEAD HARBOR PARK

DIRECTIONS: (Port Washington, Nassau County)

Take the Long Island Expressway to exit 39N. Take Glen Cove Road north to Northern Blvd. Turn left on Nothern Blvd and head west to West Shore Drive. Turn right on West Shore Drive and head north. Hempstead Harbor Park will be on your right side.

CONDITIONS:

Hempstead Harbor Park is one of the Nassau County Parks recently opened to scuba divers. Divers will need a leisure pass and a Nassau County Diving Permit, available from the Eisenhower Park Administration Building to access this site.

According to Janice Raber, this site offers ample parking with bathrooms and a short walk to an easy water entry. It's a great place for open water training. According to Darryl Steinhauser, the best diving is found on the north end of the park. Maximum depth is about 20 feet and the bottom composition is a mix of small rocks, sand and in some areas mud. Divers should note that the Pier is used frequently by fisherman. If diving under or near the pier, be very careful of encounters with lost monofilament line and fishing hooks.

HORTON POINT

DIRECTIONS: (Southold, Suffolk County)

Take the Long Island Expressway east to Exit 73, Old Country Road. Drive east on Old Country Road; it will change into Main Road. Once into the town of Southold, turn left onto Youngs Avenue. Drive north on Youngs Avenue to the end. Turn right onto North Road, then a quick left on Lighthouse Road.

Photo by Daniel Berg

Those who explore *Horton Point* will find an abundant array of marine life. Photo by Daniel Berg.

Photo by Pete Nawrocky

Lighthouse Road will bring you into a parking lot that overlooks *Horton Point Beach*. The parking lot is posted "No Parking 10p.m. to 7a.m."

CONDITIONS:

Located on the north side of the north fork, *Horton Point* is a truly unique dive site. Unfortunately, the uniqueness of the *Point* comes from how difficult it is for divers to get themselves and their dive gear into the water. To better explain, the parking lot is on top of a bluff, and there are 121 grueling steps down an old wooden staircase to get to the beach. After the dive, this hike becomes even worse when you have to lug your water-soaked dive gear back up.

For those who dive the *Point*, they will find a small pebble and sand bottom, large rocks with many crevices, an abundant array of marine life, and, of course, great lobstering!

Once back in the parking lot, divers might want to visit the Horton Point Lighthouse Marine Museum. George Washington originally commissioned the lighthouse back in 1790. The museum, maintained by the Southold Historical Society, is an enjoyable way to finish off the day.

ISLAND PARK BEACH

DIRECTIONS: **(Island Park, Nassau County)**

Take the Southern State Pkwy to Exit 20 South (Grand Ave). Stay on Grand to Sunrise Hwy and turn right. Go west on Sunrise to Long Beach Rd then turn left. Stay on Long Beach Rd south into Island Park. Take right fork and stay on Long Beach Rd. Go one block past Parma and make a right.

Island Park Beach. Photo by Daniel Berg

By using a metal detector the author recovered this gold ring and assortment of brass beach tags. Note that each year the tags have a different size and shape. Photo by Dan Berg

Note: Parking is private and can be a problem at this site. Although street parking is possible, many times the gates to this little beach are locked. Access to this site is best by boat.

CONDITIONS:

This little town beach, located on Hog Island Channel, is great for those who use underwater metal detectors to hunt for coins and jewelry. The beach is only accessible during the off-season when the beach is closed to swimmers. The beach starts out very shallow but then drops off quickly to around 20 feet. In season, swim races with lanes are set up between the main pier and a floating dock to the south. It is here that we have found a variety of brass whistles, old brass beach tags and several gold rings. Please note that the bottom is a little silty but for an experienced diver with a metal detector the current usually carries away silt and makes target location possible.

JONES BEACH JETTY

DIRECTIONS: (Jones Beach, Nassau County)

The jetty at Jones Beach is located in a state park and therefore cannot be reached from shore. The only legal way to dive this jetty is by boat. For those

Jones Beach Jetty. Photo by Daniel Berg.

Photo by Randi Eisen

who have a boat, I will give three suggestions: 1) Plan your dive at slack tide. 2) Pick a calm day. 3) Bring a spotter experienced in handling your boat.

CONDITIONS:

Getting here is only half the fun. The currents that whip through Jones Inlet can be, to say the very least, extremely strong. Only experienced divers should plan to dive here, and even then only at slack tide.

According to my old friend and dive partner, Rick Schwarz, this is one of the best jetty dives on the Island. Both day and night dives on the jetty are very productive. Lobsters and many other types of marine life are abundant. Divers can sometimes see schools of baitfish glide by or observe a small skate or sand shark while exploring the jetty.

Plan to dive the east, or beach side of the jetty. This side is sheltered from most of the inlet's currents, but as divers approach the point, they will definitely feel the current's force increasing. Do not dive on the inlet side unless you are at full slack, and even then, make sure your exit is planned before the tide turns and its' force increases. Remember that it's not a lot of fun to be carried out to sea or even into the bay. As with other current dives, knowledge of how tides and currents work is invaluable and should not be overlooked.

KENNY'S ROAD BEACH

DIRECTIONS: (Southold, Suffolk County)

Take the Long Island Expressway to Exit 73, Old Country Road. Drive east on Old Country, which will change into Main Road. Continue driving east into the town of Southold and turn left on Ackerly Pond Lane. Drive north to the end

Kennys Road Beach. Photo by Daniel Berg

and turn right on Middle Road. Turn left on Kenny Road and drive to the end.

>   *Note: The main parking lot is posted, "No Parking 10 p.m. to 7 a.m." but for divers who would like to visit this site at night, there is a dirt lot next to the paved lot, which is not posted.*

CONDITIONS:

The parking lot is no more than 30 feet from the water's edge. This is very desirable for those of us who are tired of having to walk for a long time to find decent diving.

Don't plan on filling your catch bag with lobsters. Just casually swim and explore the area. There are some large rocks in about 15 feet of water plus a good assortment of north shore marine life, including fluke and flounder in season, crabs, shrimp, schools of spearing, snappers, and even an occasional striped bass. This is also a good place for underwater photographers to practice macro photography.

The overall dive conditions are not fantastic, but for a nice relaxing, enjoyable dive, *Kenny's Road Beach* is quite nice.

LAKE RONKONKOMA

DIRECTIONS: (Lake Ronkonkoma, Suffolk County)

Take the Long Island Expressway to Exit 59. Make the second left off the service road to Pond Road, which will turn into Lake Shore Road. Lake Shore runs along the lake, and parking can be found in a few spots.

Lake Ronkonkoma

Aerial photograph of *Lake Ronkonkoma.*
Photo courtesy Photo Gramtree Branch, National Ocean Service.

CONDITIONS:

I would not recommend *Lake Ronkonkoma* to many divers. The mud bottom here reduces visibility to zero as soon as it is disturbed. I have only done two dives here. One was recreational, and I didn't see or find anything that would make me want to return. The second, was to assist the Ronkonkoma Fire Department in a search and recovery drill for its scuba team.

The lake is, however, enjoyed by some divers during winter months. Experienced ice divers enjoy cutting a hole in the winter ice and then dropping through. These divers usually find great visibility since they are suspended above the silty bottom. A word of caution: ice diving is not for all divers. It requires specialized skills and should not be attempted without the proper equipment and professional training.

A few years ago a drought caused the lakes water level to fall. Local treasure hunters flocked to the site. Now able to wade out further than ever before they recovered quite a few gold rings and lots of old coins. Divers who utilize metal detectors can still take advantage of the lake and they don't even need drought conditions to access the most lucrative sites.

For recreational diving without a metal detector, during the normal spring to fall season, *Lake Ronkonkoma* offers divers little more than an opportunity to rinse salt off of their dive gear.

The author looks out over *Laurel Lake*. Photo by Mike McMeekin.

Photo by Pete Nawrocky

LAUREL LAKE

DIRECTIONS: (Southold, Suffolk County)

NOTE: Diving is presently not permitted at this site. I'm going to give basic directions and dive site conditions just in case the situation changes in the future.

Take the Long Island Expressway to Exit 73 East, Old Country Road. Take this east into the town of Laurel. Old Country will have changed into Main Road. Turn left onto Laurel Lake Drive, which is a small dirt road. If you drive under the train trestle, you have missed Laurel Lake Drive.

CONDITIONS:

When diving was permitted, this was a good site to enjoy the fresh water environment. Divers could observe all types of fresh water marine life, including bass, trout, perch, catfish and freshwater clams. The lake, which encompasses approximately 25 acres, reaches a depth of about 40 feet. The water is always cold, so even during the summer, a full wet suit or dry suit is needed.

Aside from fish watching and the lake's ability to cleanse dive gear of salt water, bottle collectors often used the lake's silty bottom as one of their prime hunts. By reaching their arms deep into the mud bottom, often only yards from shore, divers have discovered an interesting array of ancient local bottles.

55

Long Beach in Noyack. Photo by Mike McMeekin.

LONG BEACH NOYACK

DIRECTIONS: (Southampton, Suffolk County)

Take Southern State Parkway to Exit 44 East, Sunrise Highway. Take Sunrise out past the Hamptons to the end, where it will turn into County Road No. 39. Make a left on Majors Path and drive north to the end. Turn right on Noyack Road and drive east until Noyack Road splits. Bear left on Noyack Long Beach Road, which will parallel Noyack Bay. There are parking lots on the left side. We usually pass these and park on the left side of the road. There will be some large rocks to climb down and a small beach.

CONDITIONS:

Located on the north side of the south fork, this dive site is popular for novice divers. Access is easy since parking is only a few steps from the water, and when the winds are favorable, visibility can be fantastic. Divers can usually find good visibility because the beach is sheltered on three sides. The only time I've had bad visibility was when it was caused by a strong northwest wind.

Once in the water, divers will find a mixed bottom composition of sand, pebble and rock with some medium sized rocks scattered around. Offshore a bit are dense mussel beds and at least one sunken row boat. I have always noticed a lot of fluke, flounder, crabs, scallops and mussels, but never too many lobsters.

According to scuba instructors, Ed and Jeanne Tiedemann, the depth of water averages ten to 15 feet with a 20-foot max. During the spring months, divers should expect an algae bloom, and many jellyfish. Currents are not a problem, but divers should be aware of the mild tidal drift, otherwise they might have a long walk back to their car.

I've heard rumors that dolphins can sometimes be seen from the beach, and that somewhere offshore there are unarmed torpedoes. The torpedoes were tested in World War II and never recovered. During the dives that I've made here I haven't been able to confirm either, but I do recommend *Long Beach* for those looking for a nice relaxing dive.

LUCE LANDING

DIRECTIONS: (Northville, Suffolk County)

Take the Long Island Expressway east to Exit 73, Old Country Road. Drive east through the traffic circle, and make a left on Northville Turnpike. Drive north to the end, and turn right on Sound Road. Turn left on Pier Avenue and drive north for .8 miles. Parking is posted, "By Permit Only".

CONDITIONS:

Located on the north shore, *Luce Landing* is a nice area to explore. The shallow water allows divers time to enjoy the underwater environment while slowly swimming down the beach. There are some large rocks offshore where the amount of marine life is highly concentrated. These are definitely worth a visit.

I'm told that a little further east there are two small jetties that once had a pier between them. These jetties sound like a good place for exploration, but are definitely too far to swim or walk to. Other parking would have to be found a little closer.

Luce Landing. Photo by Daniel Berg

Makamah provides divers with a nice leisurely north shore dive. Photo by Daniel Berg

MAKAMAH

DIRECTIONS: (Huntington, Suffolk County)

Take the Long Island Expressway to Exit 52 North, Commack Road. This will change names and eventually turn into Bread and Cheese Hollow Road. Turn left onto Fort Salonga Road, then make a right turn onto Makamah Road and take it to the end.

NOTE: There might be some parking problems at this site. In the past the small parking lot at the end of Fort Salonga Road was available, but I've heard that now it is closed.

CONDITIONS:

According to local divers, this location doesn't offer too much in the way of aquatic life, but it can serve as a good warm-up dive after the winter.

If legal parking can be found, divers can find some big rocks about 100 to 150 yards offshore. These boulders can be found by swimming on a 70-degree compass course where they will be exposed at low tide, and submerged at high. This area is definitely the best shot divers have at finding lobsters. In between these scattered boulders, a clean sand bottom, some bottom fish and crabs can usually be found. Boat traffic is heavy, but is usually concentrated out past the rocks and poses little danger to inshore diving.

Overall, this site is nice for a leisurely dive on the north shore, but aquatic activity is minimal.

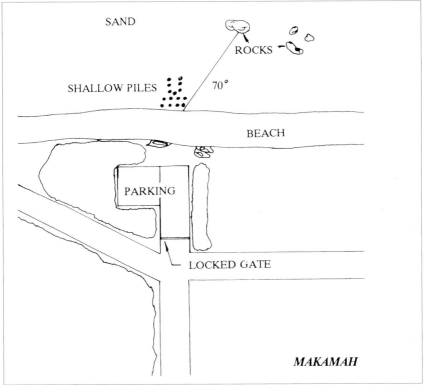

SAND

ROCKS

SHALLOW PILES   70°

BEACH

PARKING

LOCKED GATE

MAKAMAH

Sketch courtesy Kevin Travell.

MANHATTAN BEACH REEF

DIRECTIONS: (Brooklyn, Kings County)

Take the Belt Parkway to Coney Island Avenue South. Turn left on Neptune Avenue, then right on West End Avenue. Turn left on Oriental Boulevard, then right on Dover Street. Take Dover South to the end and park.

CONDITIONS:

Located on Long Island's south shore, *Manhattan Beach* offers divers living on the west end a nice local beach dive. According to Instructor, Bob Lyons, depth of water here ranges from twelve feet at low tide to 20 feet at high.

Divers can navigate to a submerged reef located just offshore by navigating on a 180-degree course for about 150 yards. Once on the reef, divers can hunt for lobsters, spear fish, or even take photographs of the wide variety of local marine life. This marine life includes starfish, anemones, crabs, fluke, flounder, black fish, and even sea urchins.

There is a running current, so dives should be planned for slack tide. Also,

59

Divers can navigate to a submerged reef located just offshore. Photo by Daniel Berg.

Photo by Pete Nawrocky.

because of the seasonal boat traffic and fishermen sporting this site, divers should be well practiced in underwater navigation. This skill will allow divers to visit the reef and return to shore without ever coming to the surface, therefore eliminating most of the danger from passing boats. The trusty dive flag also will play an important role in safely enjoying the undersea environment located at the *Manhattan Beach Reef.*

MATTITUCK TWIN JETTIES

DIRECTIONS: (Southold, Suffolk County)

WEST JETTY: Take the Long Island Expressway to Exit 73, Old Country Road. Old Country will change names to Main Road. Drive east until you pass under a train trestle, then drive .8 miles and turn left on Factory Avenue. Take Factory to the end and turn left. Drive through Middle Road and make the first right on Cox Neck Road, then left on Luthers (Breakwater) Road. Continue all the way to the end and park.

EAST JETTY: Take Old Country Road, which will merge into Main Road. Turn left onto Wickham Avenue. Make a left onto Mill Lane, then another left on East Mill or Oregon, and then right onto Reeve Avenue. Make a left turn on

Aerial photograph of *Mattituck Twin Jetties*. Photo by Daniel Berg.

Photo by Pete Nawrocky.

Baile Beach Road, and take it to the end. Parking is available on either side of the two jetties.

CONDITIONS:

I have always had good luck at this site. Visibility can be very good, but it can also be very bad. No matter what the visibility, I've found more than enough aquatic life to keep me occupied. Lobstering, of course, is always high on a beach diver's list of dive objectives. I don't think anyone will be disappointed, but lobsters have been a little scarce here for the past few years.

Overall, I prefer the *East Jetty*. Spear fishing for black fish out by the point can be very rewarding. As is the case with all inlets, divers should be aware of the currents and the heavy boat traffic during summer months.

MONTAUK TWIN JETTIES

DIRECTIONS: (Montauk, Suffolk County)

WEST JETTY: Take Southern State Parkway to Exit 44 East, Sunrise Highway. Stay on Sunrise to Montauk Highway and continue east into the town

The *Twin jetties* at Montauk are truly one of the best beach dives on Long Island. Both east and west jetties are easily accessible and both are thriving with all types of marine life. Aerial photo by Daniel Berg.

Photo by Pete Nawrocky.

of Montauk. Turn left onto Edgemere Street and drive north to the end. It will have merged into West Lake Drive.

EAST JETTY: Take Southern State Parkway to Exit 44 East, Sunrise Highway. Stay on Sunrise to Montauk Highway and continue east past the town of Montauk. Continue on Montauk Highway to East Lake Drive. Drive north on East Lake to the end.

CONDITIONS:

The *Twin Jetties* at Montauk are truly one of the best beach dive sites on Long Island. Both *East* and *West Jetties* are easily accessible, and both are popular with local divers. Divers will find all types of marine life thriving in and around the large stones. These stones act as a fish haven and provide a solid home on the otherwise empty sand bottom.

Depth of water ranges from five to 25 feet at high tide. According to most local divers with whom I have talked, either the west side of the *West Jetty*, or out by the point of the *West Jetty* are the best potential hunting grounds for spear fishing. The *East Jetty* seems to be the better site for lobstering.

I have also had excellent reports from night divers who never seem to stop raving about the abundance and variety of marine life they have observed at the *Montauk Twin Jetties*.

Photo by Daniel Berg

MORICHES JETTY

DIRECTIONS: (Fire Island, Suffolk County)

NOTE: A four-wheel-drive vehicle, and a Suffolk County Beach Permit is needed to access this site.

Take the Long Island Expressway to Exit 68 South, William Floyd Parkway. Drive south to the end (7.8 miles) and turn left onto Fire Island Beach Road. Drive as far east as you can. It's at least five miles over soft sand before you get to the jetty.

CONDITIONS:

Since only divers with four-wheel-drive vehicles or boats can get to this jetty, conditions are unspoiled. Located on the inlet's west side, the jetty's depth of water ranges from about five to 25 feet. On the northwest end, divers can explore submerged rocks, which, in the words of Captain Steve Bielenda, "make a fantastic beach dive". As with other south shore inlets, divers should realize that a strong current is present at all but slack tides.

Divers who plan to get here by boat should be aware that Moriches Inlet is closed to boating, so access is only available from the bay side.

I would only recommend this site to divers experienced in working in and around strong currents. Keep an eye on the wind, weather and tide. Picking a day to dive this site based on the best overall conditions will give you the best chance to truly enjoy this slightly remote but fascinating jetty.

Mike McMeekin walks up the beach after diving the *Murphy Wreck*. Photo by Daniel Berg

MURPHY WRECK

DIRECTIONS: **(New Suffolk, Suffolk County)**

Take the Long Island Expressway to Exit 73 East. This will be Old Country Road. Continue until you get to the town of Cutchogue. Old Country will have changed names to Route 25, or Main Road. Make a right turn onto New Suffolk Road. Drive for one mile and make the first left on Old Harbor Road and take this to the end.

CONDITIONS:

Finding this wreck site is simple. Enter the water directly in front of Old Harbor Road and swim straight out for about 50 feet.

This unidentified wreck, called the *Murphy* is said to be that of an old wood-hulled, iron framed, pleasure craft probably sunk in the early 1900's. According to a local old timer, whom we met at the site one day, the *Murphy* was converted into a barge to haul potatoes. She was finally beached and stripped of her machinery when she was of no more use.

The scattered, seaweed-covered wreckage is spread over a large area. Although very shallow (only two to four feet at low tide), this dive should be of particular interest to artifact hunters. Brass spikes and copper nails are commonplace and have been recovered easily over the years by divers who have patience, a good eye for brass, or just plain old good luck.

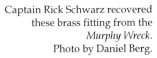

Captain Rick Schwarz recovered
these brass fitting from the
Murphy Wreck.
Photo by Daniel Berg.

OBI BEACH

DIRECTIONS: (Oak Beach, Suffolk County)

Take Southern State Pkwy to Robert Moses Pkwy and head south. Stay on
Robert Moses over the bridge than head west on Ocean Pkwy. You will have to
drive west to the first "U" turn than take Ocean Pkwy. back east towards
Captree. Get into far right lane and turn off into Oak Beach. Turn right onto the
service road and head west again. You will be traveling parallel to Ocean Pkwy.
Parking lot will be down a bit on your left side.

Photo by Daniel Berg.

Photo by Randi Eisen

Please note that the parking lot is posted "For Town Residence Only". Even though parking has not been a problem in the past, it is definitely a park at your own risk area.

CONDITIONS:

This little beach offers easy parking, excellent visibility and a gradual sloping bottom. Many area dive shops actually use the spot for their open water training sessions. Diver, Ed Slater reports that to the right of the parking lot is a patch of eel grass. It's here that divers with a good eye for detail can usually spot sea horses. On the east side of the parking lot, straight out of the small jetty, divers will find the remains of an old wooden barge. The best time to dive here is at High Slack.

U.S.S. OHIO

DIRECTIONS: (Greenport, Suffolk County)

Take the Long Island Expressway to Exit 73 East, Old Country Road. Take this all the way into the town of Greenport. Old Country Road will have changed into Route 25. Turn right onto 4th Street, and then left onto Clark Street. Take this to the end and park.

CONDITIONS:

The *U.S.S. Ohio* was built in 1817, and was launched from the Brooklyn Navy Yard on May 20, 1820. She was 208 feet long, had a 53-foot beam and was

The *U.S.S. Ohio* was built in 1817, and was launched from the Brooklyn Navy Yard in 1820.

The *U.S.S. Ohio* wreck site. Photo by Daniel Berg.

The author uses a float to
mark the *Ohio*
wreck site.
Photo by Jozef Koppelman.

classified as a 74-gun ship. The *Ohio* sat in mothballs for eighteen years and
was not commissioned until October 11, 1838. The *Ohio* became Commodore
Isaac Hull's flagship. She patrolled the Mediterranean for two years. In 1847,
when the war with Mexico broke out, the *Ohio* landed marines in Vera Cruz.
After the war ended, the *Ohio* sailed to the west coast and provided protection
to the newly acquired California territory. On September 27, 1883, after 63
years of faithful duty the *Ohio* was sold to Israel L. Snow of Rockland, Maine.
Later, the *Ohio* was sold for scrap, which is how she ended up in Greenport. In
April of 1884, after being almost completely stripped, the *Ohio* broke from her
mooring during a storm and stranded at Fanning Point. The *Ohio* was then
burned to the water line in order to reduce the wreckage from protruding
through the ocean's surface.

It was not until 1973, that local divers re-discovered the *Ohio's* remains. The
divers who found the site belonged to a branch of the British Sub Aqua Club.
They wanted to keep the site secret and off limits to other divers as they planned
to raise her artifacts and donate them to a marine museum. Shortly after locating
the wreck it was learned that Mobil Oil Company of Greenport was planning to
install groups of pilings, called dolphins, for their oil barges. These dolphins
(poles) were to be installed directly through the wreck site. The Sub Aqua Club
protested and in doing so gave away the wreck's general location.

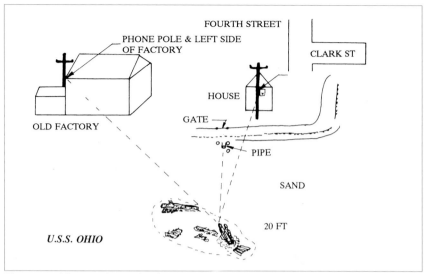

This is our old triangulation sketch of the *Ohio* wreck site. Unfortunately, the factory shown in the drawing has been torn down and replaced with condominiums. Finding the wreck now can be a little tricky. Sketch by Daniel Berg.

Captain Steve Bielenda started his own search for the wreck. After finding the *Ohio's* remains he returned to shore. Bielenda was then confronted by local police. The police and Village Board wanted to keep the site off limits to all but Sub Aqua divers. Bielenda later contested in court and won the right for recreational sport divers to dive the *Ohio* by showing that the wreck site was outside of Greenport municipal boundaries and therefore not under the jurisdiction of the board.

Today, the remains of the *Ohio* are mostly broken and buried. The small amount of wood that remains above the sand is full of wormholes and almost soft to the touch.

Finding the remains of the *U.S.S. Ohio* can be a little tricky. From Clark Street, walk along the water's edge around the bend. There will be the remains of an old iron bulkhead. Look on the waterside of this bulkhead for a pipe and some short poles. They are located directly in front of the gate in the chain link fence. Use this as a starting point. I usually swim straight out from this point until I reach a depth of 20 to 25 feet, and then I swim west, staying in this depth range until I find the wreck. If that doesn't work, I have drawn a triangulation map of the shoreline view from directly above the *Ohio*. Unfortunately, the old factory, part of my original bearings, has been torn down and replaced by condominiums. Once underwater, identifying the wreck site is most easily done by finding the remaining submerged dolphins, which were imbedded through the wreck by Mobil Oil Company. Divers can still find brass spikes from the wreck, but they are getting fewer and further between.

The *Old Ferry Pier* is located on Reynolds Channel at the mouth of Snake Creek. This dive is very shallow and divers should be aware of the powerful current that sweeps through the area .

Mike McMeekin with bottles from the *Old Ferry Pier*.

Photos by Daniel Berg

OLD FERRY PIER

DIRECTIONS: (Lawrence, Nassau County)

NOTE: There is presently no available parking at this site. The only access is by boat.

Take Sunrise Highway into the town of Lynbrook. Turn south on Broadway, then left onto Causeway Road. Turn left on Seaview Avenue and take it to the end. It turns right and changes names to Oxford. Oxford then turns left and becomes Prospect Place, which will bring you to a private yacht club. Again, no parking is permitted, but I will describe the dive for those who can find access by boat or other means.

CONDITIONS:

In 1982 my diving buddy, Rick Schwarz, and I dove this site after an old map showed us the location of a ferry pier. I was able to get permission from the yacht club, and we soon found ourselves along with other dive buddies, recovering hundreds of old blob top bottles dating back to the late 1800's. During every dive, each of us would literally fill two nylon bags with everything from beer to medicine bottles.

The remains of the pier are located at the entrance to Snake Creek on Reynolds Channel. The water is very shallow. At high tide it ranges from only two feet to eight feet, and at low tide there is hardly enough water to swim in. There is also a very strong current that whips around the point, constantly burying and uncovering bottles. When diving here we wear a little extra weight and bring a small garden type claw. This claw not only serves as a digging tool, but helps to hold ourselves in position against the current.

In 1991, Rick and I, along with divers, Mel Brenner and Mike McMeekin, returned to the *Old Ferry Pier.* We were pleasantly surprised to find that bottles could still be found. It wasn't like the old days when at the end of the dive it was hard to carry the full bag of bottles, but the site was still productive. One should note that most of the remaining bottles are buried, and probing or digging in the sand is required to locate them.

OLD PONQUOGUE BRIDGE

DIRECTIONS: (Ponquogue, Suffolk County)

Take Sunrise Highway to Exit 65 South. Make a left onto Montauk Highway, then a right turn onto Ponquogue Avenue. Take this to the end and make a left on Shinnecock Avenue. Turn left on Foster Avenue, which will bring you to the new bridge. Drive over the new bridge to the end of the road and make a U-turn onto the service road. Parking can be found on the southeast side of the old bridge in a dirt parking lot. If you want to dive the north side I would recommend dropping off your gear, then parking in the same lot and walking back.

CONDITIONS:

The *Old Ponquogue Bridge* was replaced a few years back with a larger concrete bridge. The *Old Bridge* has been left intact. This was done not only so the *Old Bridge* would serve as a platform for fishing and diving, but so it could continue to act as a valuable fish haven. Hopefully, this bridge will be left intact for sportsmen to enjoy for years to come.

Because of the strong current, this dive should only be done at slack tide, with high slack preferred. Start on the south side of the bridge where an easy entry can be made. Divers should wade along the *Old Bridge's* bulkhead until the end. Once here, smart divers wait for slack tide before beginning their descent. Divers can swim through and between the wood and concrete pilings, search for lobsters, spear black fish, gather a bag full of mussels, photograph the underwater environment, or just enjoy diving at its finest.

Be sure to keep track of the tide. Once it begins to turn, the dive should end. The current, as I mentioned before, is very strong during an incoming or outgoing tide. If a diver does get caught, it is best not to swim against it. The intelligent diver, who knows how currents work, will float with it until it starts to dissipate and then swim to shore at an angle. For the beginner, I would

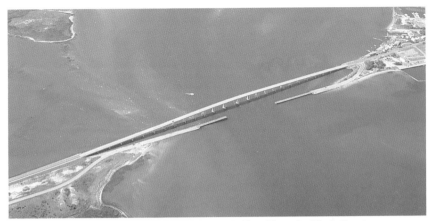

Aerial photo of both the *Old* and *New Ponquoque Bridges*. Photo by Hank Garvin.

Photo by Pete Nawrocky

Photo by Daniel Berg

always recommend an advanced diving course. An advanced diving course will not only be beneficial for this site, but will enhance all basic diving skills, so that all dives can be enjoyed to their fullest.

Diving the north side of the bridge, divers will find more of the same plus some. Since a long walk is required, diving is less common here and legal size lobsters are more abundant.

Whether diving the north side or the south side, be sure not to swim past the halfway point, since it is illegal to swim or dive in the channel. The halfway point can be easily recognized while underwater by a concrete wall. Just don't swim around it, and you'll be fine.

Ponquogue's New Bridge, located just west of the *Old Bridge* has already become another good dive site. Local divers are already enjoying the thriving fish haven under this recently built structure.

In 1996, The *Old Bridge* was in desperate need of repair. Southampton Town was short of funds. They turned to New York State who agreed to help finance the project but insisted that a boat ramp be installed. Unfortunately, the only place to put the ramp was between the two bridges. The ramp's location and the associated boat traffic would cause major problems to divers. In 1998, as the renovation project was nearing completion, Randy Randazzo from the Hampton Dive Center, along with members of the Long Island Divers Association organized numerous meeting with Southampton Town and New York State officials. Thanks to their effort, the boat channel was routed around the dive area and the first underwater marine park in Southampton Town was formed.

Today, the site is still one of the best on Long Island. Southampton Town residents can park with a seasonal beach sticker on their vehicle. Non-residents can purchase an annual bridge-parking sticker. Stickers can be obtained Monday through Friday directly from the town (631) 282-6000 or on weekends from Hampton Dive Center.

PARADISE COVE

DIRECTIONS: (Freeport, Nassau County)

Take Meadowbrook State Parkway to Merrick Road west. Turn left onto Mill Road to the end and turn left onto South Main Street. Turn right onto Atlantic Ave. and head west. Turn left on Miller Ave. and drive south to the end. Parking is available along the side the road. The dive site can be reached by climbing over the bulkhead at the end of Miller Ave.

Paradise Cove is a typical south shore bay dive.
Photo by Captain Rick Schwarz.

Photo by Pete Nawrocky

CONDITIONS:

Paradise Cove is a typical south shore bay dive. The bottom composition here is comprised of mud and clay close to shore and then turns to a crushed shell and sand bottom further out. Maximum depth is approximately 15 feet and visibility at high tide can be better than ten feet. According to Doug Pettit divers will not only see many big yellow and red sponges, but the area is also well known for the abundance of sea horses. Doug also recommends that divers bring a ladder with them to make climbing up and down the bulk heading easy.

ROANOKE POINT BARGES

DIRECTIONS: (Reeves Park, Suffolk County)

NOTE: A four -wheel-drive vehicle plus a beach permit will be necessary to get to these wrecks.

Take the Long Island Expressway into Riverhead - Exit 73 East. Take Old Country Road east and make a left at the traffic circle onto Roanoke Avenue. Take Roanoke Avenue to Sound Avenue and make a left. Turn right on Park Road and take it to the end. The barges are about .6 miles down the beach to the west.

CONDITIONS:

There are actually two dive sites here. Those without a four-wheel-drive vehicle can dive on the rocks at the end of Park Road. The rest of us who have

The submerged barge wrecks off *Roanoke* can be found by swimming due north from this barge which sits on the beach. Photo courtesy Captain Steve Bielenda.

Captain Steve Bielenda
stands next to one of
Roanokes self propelled barges
Photo courtesy Steve Bielenda.

a four-wheel-drive vehicle, or who are willing to thumb a ride down the beach to the west, can dive a truly beautiful spot. All of the wrecks here are self-propelled barges that ran aground during a winter storm. To find the wrecks, use the two exposed barges on the beach as landmarks. From these barges, swim north for about 100 yards.

According to Instructor, Charlie Orlowski, the depth of water is about 25 feet, and the lobstering is great. The submerged barges with their large, steel, four-blade propellers make a nice background for underwater photographs.

If you have never been to the *Barge Wrecks,* or as they are also known, the *Reeves Beach Barges,* you should definitely put them high on your list of future beach dives. These wrecks seem to be an oasis in the middle of a barren desert. Their presence serves as a fish haven, and all types of aquatic life have made their home in and around the *Roanoke Point Barges*.

ROCKY POINT EAST

DIRECTIONS: **(East Marion, Suffolk County)**

Take the Long Island Expressway East to Exit 73, Old Country Road. Drive east on Old Country Road through the traffic circle and make a left on Northville Turnpike. Drive north to the end and turn right on Sound Avenue.

Rocky Point is east end beach
diving at its finest.
Photo by Daniel Berg.

Sound Avenue will become Middle Road. Take this east until you see a sign for East Marion; turn left onto Rocky Point Road. Drive north to the end and park. Parking is not allowed at the end of Rocky Point Road between 10 p.m. and 7 a.m. Other parking will have to be found if you're planning to dive within these hours.

CONDITIONS:

Rocky Point is east end beach diving at its' finest. The pebble beach leads into a clean sand and rock bottom. The depth of the water is about 15 to 20 feet, and a mild tidal drift is usually present. Divers will enjoy fantastic visibility of up to 25 feet if the wind and waves are right. The large rocks that are located just offshore not only provide homes for lobsters, but also attract porgy and nice size black fish.

A word of caution: the beach is at the bottom of a bluff, so divers will have to climb or walk down approximately 20 feet of sand and loose rocks. Be careful, since this path is difficult for all, especially when fully suited in dive gear.

ROCKY POINT LANDING

DIRECTIONS: (Rocky Point, Suffolk County)

Take the Long Island Expressway to Exit 63 North, Patchogue Road. Drive north to the end and make a right. Drive east to Hallock Landing Road and make a left. Bear left onto Rocky Point Landing Road, which will turn into Hagerman Landing Road. Take this to the end. There is no parking allowed, so divers will have to arrange to be dropped off or find another entrance point.

CONDITIONS:

Rocky Point Landing has, as the name implies, plenty of rocks. According to local divers, the rocks that lie just offshore are a great haven for lobsters. Divers

Photo by Daniel Berg

will find a clean white sand bottom with an abundance of typical north shore marine life, like fluke, flounder, porgies, hermit crabs, spider crabs and starfish. Spear fishermen can enjoy the occasional sighting of a good size black fish, or the plentiful selection of bottom fish. This site is also good for underwater photography.

RODA WRECK

DIRECTIONS: (Tobay, Nassau County)

Take the Southern State Parkway to Wantagh State Parkway south. Drive south on Wantagh to Ocean Parkway east. Drive east to Tobay Beach. The wreck is located directly offshore of Tobay Beach.

CONDITIONS:

Built by A. McMillan & Son, Ltd; Dumbarton in 1897, and owned by the C.T. Bowring & Company, the *Roda* was 315 feet long by 44 feet wide. She displaced 2,516 tons and was powered by a 263-nhp triple expansion engine.

On February 13, 1908, while on a voyage from Huelva, Spain, to New York, carrying a full cargo of copper ore, the *Roda* was driven aground by an icy eastern gale onto what is now known as Tobay Beach. All of the Roda's crew were saved in what was called "The most heroic rescue on the Long Island coast in the winter of 1908".

The *Roda* broke in two shortly after running aground, thus spilling her cargo

The *Roda Wreck*. Photo courtesy Suffolk Marine Museum, Sayville, New York.

into the sea. She remained visible for a few years until a storm broke her rusted skeleton and finally sent her to the ocean floor.

Today, the *Roda* rests in 20 to 30 feet of water, one-quarter mile offshore. Her twisted remains and cargo are spread all over the seabed. As far as diving this wreck, the surge in this area requires some experience, yet, on a calm day and for a strong swimmer, she is within swimming distance from the beach. I have to recommend that diving the *Roda* be accomplished by boat. I have included the wreck in this text only because some divers have successfully reached the wreck from shore. I have only visited this wreck by boat and have only anchored over this site twice. Each time I found that not more than five feet from my boat was wreckage that came within inches of the surface. If you want to dive or fish over this site, I highly recommend using extreme care and caution.

RYE CLIFF FERRY WRECK

DIRECTIONS: (Sea Cliff, Nassau County)

Take the Long Island Expressway to Exit 39, Glen Cove Road North. This will change names to Cedar Swamp Road. Proceed north until the end and make a left turn onto Glen Cove Avenue. Make a right turn onto Shore Drive, which will take you along the water. At the end of this road, before Shore Drive turns to go uphill, there is a small park overlooking the Sound. Parking is available all along the south side of Shore Drive. During the summer, Shore Drive becomes a one-way street, so a small detour will have to be taken.

The *Rye Cliff Ferry Wreck.* Courtesy Steam Ship Historical Society, University of Baltimore Library.

Rye Cliff Ferry Wreck

Sea Cliff Park. Photo by Daniel Berg

Photo by Jozef Koppelman

The author recovered this small pewter trophy while metal detecting on the *Rye Cliff Ferry Wreck*. Photo by Steve Jonassen.

In 1999 the author recovered this unique diamond ring and Thailer Dollar dated 1784. Photo by Daniel Berg.

CONDITIONS:

The *Rye Cliff Ferry Wreck* was built in 1898, and named the *General Knox.* It was later sold and re-named the *Rye Cliff.* This car ferry, which was 137 feet long, burned to the water line and sank on September 28th, 1918, while at its' dock in Sea Cliff.

To find this wreck, divers should walk into the park and take a compass bearing of 230 degrees out from the telephone pole with the white sign mounted to it. Divers should then carefully climb down the rocks and swim along that course for about 50 yards. There shouldn't be too much of a problem finding the wreck since it is scattered over a very large area.

Also known as the *Sea Cliff Park Wreck*, or *Ferry Wreck*, she lies very low and is mostly sanded over. One small section protrudes up about eight feet off the bottom. In this particular spot a few black fish can usually be seen. The rest of the wreckage lies a little further offshore. Divers who visit this wreck should not expect to find too many remains, but if they look hard enough and fan around in the sand, brass spikes and other artifacts can still be found.

Back in 1986, we found the brass rudder gudgeon from the wreck. The artifact was still attached to the wreck and even after several dives would not budge. The gudgeon is still there ready to be salvaged by some ambitious diver.

In 1992, I returned to the wreck with divers, Rick Schwarz and Mike McMeekin. We were experimenting with different types of underwater metal detectors and chose this site because it was shallow, relatively calm and had decent visibility. Anyway, Rick, Mike and I soon found how productive metal detectors really can be. We each recovered 20 or so brass spikes by scanning the sand surrounding the wreck.

In 1997, a local "archeologist" claimed to have located the *Rye Cliff Ferry Wreck.* Local papers were even convinced that the story was news worthy. I found this amusing since this wreck has been listed since the very first edition of this book, back in 1986. In addition, I had actually taken this guy on a tour of the site. Please note, that I make no claim as to discovering this wreck. Its' location and history have been known to local divers since the early 1980's.

In 1999, Ed Slater, Aaron Hirsh and I were metal detecting around the wreck site. I surfaced with a variety of old coins, a gold ring and a Hungarian Thaler Dollar dated 1784. Although the coin did not come from the wreck it does indicate the age and history of the area.

SAG HARBOR JETTIES

DIRECTIONS: (Sag Harbor, Suffolk County)

Take Southern State to Sunrise Highway East. Stay on Sunrise, which will turn

Aerial photo of *Sag Harbor Jetties*. Courtesy Hank Garvin.

into Montauk Highway. Drive east into the town of Water Mill. Make a left turn onto Scuttle Hole Road and drive north to the end. Turn left on Sag Harbor Turnpike. Take the Turnpike, which turns into Main St. to the end. The only close parking is from the Yacht Club property, and permission is needed for access. The only other option is a long walk or by boat. The later is definitely the recommended way to visit these jetties.

CONDITIONS:

Diving the jetties can be quite rewarding. Both jetties are very long and at high tide visibility can be quite good. Divers have found everything from lobsters and blackfish to old bottles. *Sag Harbor* itself also can be a fascinating dive. The harbor has been used as a safe refuge since colonial times, and divers have recovered a wide assortment of bottles from the area. Remember to watch out for boat traffic and be sure to tow a dive flag.

SEA CLIFF BEACH & WATCH WRECK

DIRECTIONS: (Sea Cliff, Nassau County)

Take the Long Island Expressway to Exit 39, Glen Cove Road North, which will change into Cedar Swamp Road. Proceed north until the end and make a left turn onto Glen Cove Avenue. Make a right turn on Shore Drive, which will take you along the water's edge. About a half mile down, directly across from Sea Cliff Beach, there is a small dirt parking lot. During the fall and winter months, divers can park here and walk through the beach gate to a small jetty. This is where we begin our dives. During the summer months when the beach is open, parking can be found back at Sea Cliff Park, but this will require a decent swim. As with the *Rye Cliff Wreck* site, Shore Road becomes a one-way street during the beach season, so a small detour will have to be taken.

The *Watch Wreck* is located just offshore of this jetty.
Photo by Daniel Berg.

The author recovered
this small brass porthole
from the *Watch Wreck*.
Photo by Denise Berg.

Steve Jonassen, Bill Campbell
and the author recovered
these mooring anchors from
the *Sea Cliff
Beach* area.
Photo by Denise Berg.

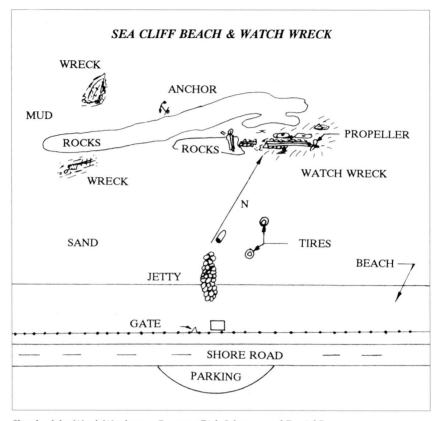

Sketch of the *Watch Wreck* area. Courtesy Rick Schwarz and Daniel Berg

CONDITIONS:

To locate the *Watch Wreck*, start at the tip of the jetty and swim a compass course due north. If you swim over a large rock bed, you have gone a little too far. The wreck lies mostly inshore but is partially mixed in with this rock bed.

The *Watch Wreck* received its' name after Steve Jonassen, a local diver, lost and then recovered his brand new diver's watch. I feel that this unidentified wreck is that of an old workboat. Most of the wreck, which I've approximated to be at least 60 feet long is buried. However, wood beams, ribs and a four-foot diameter steel propeller can still be viewed. The propeller is hard to recognize with one blade broken, and one buried, but it's located on the southeast side.

This wreck is a good place to settle down and dig. Artifacts that I have recovered include a brass water pump, a head pump; copper nails, a small brass porthole and some bottles. All date back to the early forties.

After exploring the wreck, I usually swim west along the rock bed located just offshore of the wreck, which runs parallel to shore. Two other wrecks, small cabin type crafts, can be found off this rock bed.

The whole area is good for finding old bottles and other artifacts. Although this site is not known for finding too many lobsters, I've seen at least two four-pounders caught, which isn't bad for diving off the beach.

SHELL CREEK

DIRECTIONS: (Island Park, Nassau County)

Take the Southern State Pkwy to Exit 20 South (Grand Ave). Stay on Grand to Sunrise Hwy and turn right. Go west on Sunrise to Long Beach Rd then turn left. Stay on Long Beach Rd south into Island Park. Take the left fork onto Austin Blvd. Make a left onto Empire or Nevada, then take Jamaica to the end.

Note: Parking is private and can be a problem at this site. Divers have in the past been able to utilize street parking between C&S Marina and Shell Creek Marina. One group obtained permission to use one of the boat yard parking lots. Others access the site by boat.

CONDITIONS:

Shell Creek is actually a nice protected beach dive. Located on the east side of Island Park, conditions here are not usually affected by even strong winds. I would advise diving here during an incoming or high tide for the best conditions. The bottom is silty but divers will find the remains of six small wrecks including a wood barge. According to Darryl Steinhauser, many of the wrecks, are attached together by a cable. Darryl reports that divers can find the cable by starting between C&S and Shell Creek Marinas and than just heading due south for 100'. Once the cable is located if you go east the cable will bring you to a 30' and a 20' long wreck. By heading west the cable leads to broken down wreckage. Divers should note that boat traffic in *Shell Creek* can be very heavy.

Shell Creek. Photo by Daniel Berg.

Aerial photo of the *Shinnecock Twin Jetties*. Photo courtesy Hank Garvin.

SHINNECOCK TWIN JETTIES

DIRECTIONS: **(Southampton, Suffolk County)**

WEST JETTY: Take the Long Island Expressway to Exit 65 South. Make a left on Montauk Highway, then a right on Ponquogue Avenue. Take this to the end and make a left on Shinnecock Avenue. Make a right turn on Foster Avenue. Cross over the Ponquogue Bridge and then make a left on Beach Road. Take this to the end and park in the lot named Charles F. Alterkirch Memorial Park. There is another small lot closer to the jetties, but parking is not allowed.

EAST JETTY: Take the Long Island Expressway to Exit 65 South. Make a left on Montauk Highway and drive east. Parking is limited and the walk is long. I have seen four-wheel-drive vehicles here, which definitely make things easier.

CONDITIONS:

While diving either jetty, always be sure not to dive in the inlet or on the inlet side of the jetty. This is illegal, and, if caught, fines will be given. Diving is usually done on the beach side of the *West Jetty*. I would recommend high slack tide for the best visibility. On the west side, for example, depth averages about five feet. I am told that out by the point there is a deep spot in excess of 50 feet.

I will not even try to describe all of the marine life that thrives at both of these sites, but let me just say that I have always been amazed at the variety and quantity.

This site is well known among local divers. Most first time visitors see only enough to make them want to return. So, if you do visit this site, don't expect to find a deserted jetty, but have no fear, there's room enough for all.

SHOREHAM TWIN JETTIES

DIRECTIONS: (Shoreham, Suffolk County)

Take the Long Island Expressway to Exit 69 North, Wading River Road. Take this to the end and make a left on North County Road. Take this road to the end and make a left on North Wading River Road. Make a right on Sound Road to the end. The road curves left and becomes Creek Road. Take this to the end, and you will find a small parking lot on the left side. To get to the jetties, you must swim across the creek (Wading River), and then walk. Don't let anyone fool you: it's a long walk, but well worth it. Although there is no sign, I believe that this parking lot is restricted to town residents. There are two other options: drop off your gear and park down the road, or, if you have a four-wheel-drive vehicle, there might be an access road on the west side of the power plant.

Photo by Pete Nawrocky.

Aerial photo of the *Shoreham Twin Jetties* and Nuclear Plant. In the photo you can also see the dirt parking lot and Wading River. Divers have to swim across this creek and then walk down the beach to reach the jetties. Photo by Daniel Berg.

CONDITIONS:

Shoreham is definitely a hot spot for lobstering. Over the past few years I've only found the time to dive here about fifteen times, all of which were night dives. Each dive has been rewarded by catching the limit of lobsters.

Both jetties are equally productive, although the west side of the *West Jetty* has always been a little luckier for me. Visibility at *Shoreham* always seems to be just a little better than elsewhere on Long Island, and the lack of a strong current makes for a relaxing, almost effortless dive. I have been most thankful for this, considering the length of the walk to get to and from the car.

A couple of years back, when I had planned a night dive at Shoreham, one of my dive buddies talked a friend into bringing two tanks. He figured that by doing two dives, they would catch twice as many lobsters. He was right, but neither will ever try to lug an extra tank down that beach again. They both had to literally drag themselves back to the car.

Even with the long walk, I consider the *Shoreham Jetties* to be one of the better beach dives on Long Island. Every diver should experience this site at least once.

SORE THUMB

DIRECTIONS: (Babylon, Suffolk County)

NOTE: *A four-wheel-drive vehicle or boat will be needed to reach this dive site.*

Take Southern State Parkway to Exit 40 South. Drive south on Robert Moses Causeway over two bridges and get off on Ocean Parkway West. The *Sore Thumb* is located on the left, directly opposite *Democrat Point.* Please check with local authorities for a beach permit in order to legally drive on the beach.

CONDITIONS:

The dive site is located on the west side of Fire Island Inlet. It is not, however, on the point, but rather tucked in, around the bend, in a cove on the bay or north side of the inlet. Divers will find loads of submerged rocks here with pretty decent visibility.

The current in Fire Island Inlet is usually very strong, but divers with whom I've talked say that shelter can be found by staying within the small cove. This is true as long as dives are made during the incoming tide. During an outgoing tide this cove is open to the current's force and will not shelter divers, so be sure to keep a good eye on changing conditions. Dives should be planned towards the end of the incoming tide and during high slack. The dive should be ended as soon as the tide turns to go out. Divers will want to make sure their

The *Sore Thumb* is located on the west side of Fire Island Inlet. Photo Daniel Berg.

underwater compass navigation techniques have been well practiced. It's a lot easier and much more enjoyable to navigate back to shore beneath the surface rather than to struggle with on-surface swimming.

Divers also should note that the inlet itself is very busy with boat traffic. Staying close to a diver's flag, even while within the protected cove, is a must.

SUMMERVILLE BASIN TUG

DIRECTIONS: **(Far Rockaway, Queens County)**

Take the Southern State Parkway to Exit 19 South, which is Peninsula Boulevard. Drive south on Peninsula to Rockaway Turnpike and turn left. Turn right on Burnside Avenue and take Burnside to Beach Channel Drive and just continue to head west. Turn right on 63rd Street. Head north to Elizabeth and turn right. Drive to the end and park. The wreck is at the base of Summerville Basin and is only partially submerged.

As a side note, I would like to forewarn anyone who visits this area that the neighborhood is, to say the least, not the best. One of our biggest concerns when diving here was whether or not our car would be stolen while we were underwater.

CONDITIONS:

This old abandoned tugboat sitting up on the west side of Summerville Basin was spotted one day while we were diving the *Beach 59th Street Wreck*. I decided to snorkel over and take a closer look. At first, the tugboat looked completely stripped, but once I slipped beneath the surface, I found two intact brass portholes just below the water line. The next day, my brother Dennis and I returned. After about two hours of work with a sledgehammer, chisel, crow bar and punch the portholes were free. Anyone who has ever retrieved a porthole

Summerville Basin Tug

Summerville Basin Tug

Sunken Barge

By looking closely at this aerial photograph you can see the *Summerville Basin Tug* and a sunken barge. Photo by Daniel Berg.

The author and his brother Dennis Berg recovered these portholes from the *Summerville Basin Tug.* Photo by Bill Campbell.

The author holds one of the tugs massive portholes. Photo by Dennis Berg

knows that they are mounted from the interior. We had driven the rivets in from outside the wreck. The portholes were free but I still had to go inside to retrieve them. Because the tug's bow is up on the bank, with a port list, and her stern is down in the mud penetration is a little tricky. Once inside silt quickly reduced visibility to zero. After finding the loose porthole I located the exit by feeling my way along a wall until I reached the open door space. After two such trips into the wreck, one for each porthole, we departed. I have never been back partially because I saw no other artifacts worth the effort but mainly because I have no desire to attempt such a difficult penetration again.

Ed Slater reported that only a couple of years ago another porthole, as well as a cage lamp, was recovered from the site.

THEODORE ROOSEVELT COUNTY PARK

DIRECTIONS: (Montauk, Suffolk County)

Take Montauk Highway east through Montauk Village. Continue on Montauk Highway past East Lake Drive. Park sign and entrance is on the north side of Montauk Highway.

CONDITIONS:

Janice Raber from LIDA sent me the following information on this Suffolk County Park. The outer beach is accessible with a four wheel drive vehicle and is recommended for novice and intermediate divers. Janice reports that by heading east past Shagwong Point divers can find medium sized rocks, clean white sand, good visibility and a depth of about 15 feet.

THROGS NECK JETTY

DIRECTIONS: (Whitestone,Queens County)

Take the Cross Island Parkway north to Bell Boulevard. At the end of the exit ramp make a right onto Fort Totten Avenue. Drive about a hundred yards; a dirt parking lot will be on your left just before the entrance to Fort Totten.

CONDITIONS:

The *Throgs Neck Jetty* is located between the Throgs Neck Bridge and Fort Totten. This dive site, which is definitely not one of the most popular on the island, should only be done during an incoming or high tide. Visibility at low tide is usually only a few inches, but the intelligent diver will find ten feet or more to be the norm at high slack. The bottom conditions as you swim offshore range from hard sand to mud to soft silt. Diving is best on the east side of the jetty. Debris, such as car tires, shopping carts, and beer cans, are seen on both sides. They are an unfortunate reminder of how man ruins the environment.

The *Throgs Neck Jetty* is located between the Throgs Neck Bridge and Fort Totten.
Photo by Daniel Berg

Back in 1979, when Kevin Travell
and I first explored this site,
I recovered this
beautifully preserved World
War II riffle.
Photo by Mike McMeekin.

Back in 1979, Kevin Travell and I were the first sport divers to explore this
area. We recovered all sorts of interesting artifacts. At first, old bottles were the
main prize, but soon after I found a beautifully preserved World War II rifle.
During later dives, pistols, a dagger and all types of ammunition have been
brought up. Today, divers who look hard enough can still find bullets scattered
in the sand a few feet from the jetty.

Aside from the artifacts, I have always been thrilled by the spectacular midnight
view of the Throgs Neck Bridge, as it can only be seen from water level in the

middle of Little Bay.

For hunting marine life like lobster and black fish, I would not recommend this site. Being so close to the city, I question the cleanliness of the water.

Diving instructors sometimes use this site for open water training. It offers the instructor and students close parking for many cars, a protected cove, water depth up to 25 feet and, if planned right, decent visibility.

WEAKS POINT JETTY

DIRECTIONS: (Glen Cove, Nassau County)

The pleasure of parking at or near the *Weaks Point Jetty* is basically non-existent. For those who don't mind a long walk, here are basic directions. Take the Long Island Expressway to Exit 39 North- Glen Cove Road. This will change names to Cedar Swamp Road. Proceed north until the end and make a right onto Glen Cove Avenue. Go about one-half mile and make a left onto Cottage Row. Cottage Row turns into Roosevelt at the traffic light. Make a right turn on Crescent Beach Road. Drive for .4 miles and turn left onto Valley Road. Take Valley for .7 miles, then bear left through the small gate and drive to the beach house. I have been here only a few times and have never had a problem with parking in this lot, but there is alternate parking for Glen Cove town residents at the end of Valley Road. The jetty is located a half-mile down the beach to the west. Another option would be to get to the jetty by boat.

This hook shaped jetty is truly unique and well worth all the hassles of getting here. Photo by Daniel Berg.

CONDITIONS:

This hook-shaped jetty is truly unique and well worth all the hassles it takes to get there. It is extremely long and built out of very large rocks. These rocks create cave-like homes for all types of marine life, especially crabs, eels and lobsters. Depth ranges from five to almost 30 feet out by the point, and because the jetty breaks up most wave action, good visibility can usually be found on at least one side.

For lobstering, I would recommend night dives. During the day the caves are just a little too deep, and most of the resident bugs can't even be seen. A good spear fishermen should easily be able to fill his bag while cruising over the jetty or the rock beds that cover most of the bottom on the northeast side.

Current doesn't play too much of a role when diving here, but an incoming or high slack tide is, of course, the best for water clarity.

Over the winter of 1991, Mike McMeekin and I returned to the *Weaks Point Jetty* for the first time in many years. At the base of the jetty in only a few feet of water I found a small wreck. The wreck, apparently a small inboard motorboat, must have broken free from its mooring and drifted into the jetty. Already smashed up, all that remained of this new wreck were her ribs, engine and brass propeller.

WILDWOOD LAKE

DIRECTIONS: (Riverside, Suffolk County)

Take Sunrise Highway to Exit 61 North, Moriches Riverhead Road. Stay on Moriches River Head Road to Lakeview and turn right. The lake will be on your right side. Parking is available on Lakeview.

CONDITIONS:

According to scuba instructor, Jim Cacace, *Wildwood Lake* has a bottom composition of mud and silt. The lake has a maximum depth of approximately 25 feet. Jim reports that visibility can be better than 20 feet during winter and early spring, but during the summer months reduces dramatically due to algae growth. Jim also reports that divers can usually see cray fish, small perch, and trout. Divers have also recovered a variety of bottles from the lake but nothing that was very old.

Wildwood Lake is a nice dive site for checking out equipment and fresh water photography.

Mike McMeekin looks out over *WildWood Lake* before suiting up to go diving.
Photo by Daniel Berg.

Wildwood Lake has a bottom composition of mud and silt. The lake has a maximum
depth of approximately 25 feet. This lake is great for fresh water photography.
Photo by Daniel Berg.

INDEX

INDEX

Other Books by the Author

Wreck Valley, Daniel Berg, Aqua Explorers, Inc. (1986)
Shore Diver, Daniel Berg, Aqua Explorers, Inc. (1987)
Tropical Shipwrecks, Daniel & Denise Berg, Aqua Explorers, Inc. (1989)
Wreck Valley Vol II, Daniel Berg, Aqua Explorers, Inc. (1990)
Bermuda Shipwrecks, Daniel & Denise Berg, Aqua Explorers, Inc. (1991)
Shipwreck Diving, Daniel Berg, Aqua Explorers, Inc. (1991)
Florida Shipwrecks, Daniel & Denise Berg, Aqua Explorers, Inc. (1991)
New Jersey Beach Diver, Daniel Berg, Aqua Explorers, Inc. (1993)
Long Island Shore Diver, 2nd Edition, Daniel Berg, Aqua Explorers, (1993)
SSI Wreck Diving Manual, Daniel Berg, Scuba Schools International. (1994)

Videos by the Author

DIVE WRECK VALLEY VHS Video Series (each episode 30 min)

U.S.S. San Diego, Lizzie D, Kenosha, Pinta, R.C. Mohawk, Bronx Queen, Propeller Salvage, U.S.S. Algol, U.S.S. Tarpon, Relief Ship, H.M.S. Culloden, Mistletoe, Valerie E, Algol Helm Recovery, Black Warrior, Metal Detecting, USS Tarantula, Diego 50 Cal Amo, Pilot Boat, Linda, Dual Wrecks, Brunette, Garvies Point, Iberia, Oregon, Emerald, Asfalto, Steel Wreck, Side Scan Sonar, Delaware, G&D(Yankee), Mohawk, Water Dredge, Valerie Prop Salvage, Arnoff, Dry Suit Diving, Dutch Springs, Tanks (Artifical Reef), N.E. Marine Life, Hylton Castle, Eureka, Inshore Schooner, Lizzie D Dredge, Done Deal, Bianca C(Grenada), 1000 Islands (St Lawrence River)

Other Products by the Author

#WVCD	Wreck Valley Multi Media Shipwreck CD	(NY, NJ, CT, MA)
#WVCHART	Wreck Valley Decorative Shipwreck Chart Poster	(NY&NJ)
#NCCHART	North Carolina Decorative Shipwreck Chart Poster	
#NECHART	New England Decorative Shipwreck Chart Poster	(RI to ME)
#DMVCHART	Delaware, Maryland & Virginia Shipwreck Chart Poster	
#AEDL	Aqua Explorer Waterproof Divers Log	

Patented Items

#UPB	Ultimate Pony Bracket, Patent #5,579,967 (1996)
#JLC	Jon Line Clip, Patent #5,636,413 (1997)
#IDFF	Inflatable Dive Flag/Float, Patent #5,735,719 (1998)
#UVDB	Ultimate Velcro Double Bands, Patent #5,913,467 (1999)
#QRPB	Quick Release Pony Bracket (Patent Pending 2001)

Charter Dive Boat Wreck Valley

Capt. Dan operates the 40' custom dive boat *R/V Wreck Valley.* The *Wreck Valley* runs 6-pack charters out of Jones Inlet on Long Islands south shore. From here Capt. Dan can choose from hundreds of shipwreck destinations. Check our web-site for schedule and additional information.
www.AquaExplorers.com